IMAGES
of America

GERMANTOWN

St. Boniface Catholic Church stands tall as a testament to the hard work, ingenuity, and faith of the Germans who began this settlement. The church was completed in 1854. It is a recognized landmark and is the foundation of the community. St. Boniface Catholic Church is referred to as the Mother Church of Clinton County because this church was the beginning of many Catholic parishes in the area. (Courtesy of Carolyn Beer.)

ON THE COVER: One-room schoolhouses were common in rural America. At one time, more than 12,000 one-room schools existed in Illinois alone. In this photograph, taken in the early 1920s, these happy children are ready with rakes, hoes, brooms, and tools to work at cleaning up the schoolyard at Woodlane country school. The school was located a mile and a half west of Germantown on the southwest corner of Woodlane Road and State Route 161. (Courtesy of Sue Kalmer.)

IMAGES
of America

GERMANTOWN

Mary Jansen Parrent
Foreword by Red Schoendienst

ARCADIA
PUBLISHING

Published by Arcadia Publishing
Charleston, South Carolina

Library of Congress Control Number: 2011922365

For all general information, please contact Arcadia Publishing:
Telephone 843-853-2070
Fax 843-853-0044
E-mail sales@arcadiapublishing.com
For customer service and orders:
Toll-Free 1-888-313-2665

Visit us on the Internet at www.arcadiapublishing.com

*In memory of my parents, Gerald Jansen and Margaret (Fruth) Jansen,
who nurtured my faith in God and taught me community responsibility.*

*"We travel the world over in search of what we need
and return home to find it."*

—George Moore

CONTENTS

FOREWORD

There was a basketball ring up against the barn at the Jansens, the only basketball ring that we knew of. We used to go over there and play quite a bit. Then we'd wind up there at night playing cards. The Jansen home was usually wide open. So when Mary said her name, I knew she was the daughter of the brother we called "Bisky."

I think it is great that somebody wrote this book about Germantown, and I'm just glad to be a part of it. I grew up here and my roots are still here. I can remember going fishing, and whenever it got warm enough, we went swimming down at Old Shoal Creek. We'd walk out there and swing on the grapevines.

And we used to play ball anywhere. At home, we played in the chicken yard and we would have to jump fences to catch the ball. The baseball was a rag ball that you made yourself. We made our own bats, too. When we used them, the ball wouldn't travel very far—which was good. When I was older, the man that was a big part of organizing the county league was Ed Roach. He worked with the other towns. I can still see him get up calmly and get everything organized so easily. I didn't play much, but I could see what he was doing with the rest of the team before I ever started playing. Now I see that Ed Roach was my mentor.

This is the history of Germantown—what it is now and what it was then. It will be especially good for the younger people, who weren't around here during the tough days of the Great Depression in the 1930s and 1940s, to read this book. It makes you think about people and where they are now—even the kids that I was brought up with, like Stevie Kohnen and my friend Joe Linnemann, the Wuebbels boys, and so many others.

This book will probably be hard for kids to believe when they see how things were done years back in the 1940s and before. It will also get other people talking about Germantown. The people of Germantown named the ball field after me, and I feel honored to be a part of this town's history.

—Red Schoendienst

ACKNOWLEDGMENTS

Above all else, praise and thanksgiving go to God for the constant energy, motivation, and inspiration I have received in compiling and writing this book. For providing support in so many ways, I am truly grateful to my family.

The people primarily responsible in the creation of this book are the residents and former residents of Germantown themselves. Since there is no historical society in Germantown, this book had to rely on the memories, photographs, and newspaper articles from friends and neighbors. Thank you all for your time and efforts.

Appreciation must also go to those who have written articles, books, and booklets commemorating the anniversaries and history of Germantown. Your efforts were extremely important in writing this book and will continue to be referenced by many throughout our town's history.

The older residents of our town are truly a valuable resource and deserve recognition. Thanks to all of you for welcoming me into your homes and sharing your memories, stories, knowledge, and a few laughs. And thank you for always being available to answer my questions.

Cindy Zurliene, principal of Germantown Elementary School, Vicky Albers, editor of the *Breese Journal*, and Msgr. Fr. Jim Buerster, pastor of St. Boniface Catholic Church, have all been instrumental in getting the word out about this book to the community and county. Your efforts are greatly appreciated.

Special thanks go to Eric Deering, Eric Essington, Kelly Stukenburg, Melinda Knobeloch, Bette Fawley, and everyone at the Germantown Village Hall.

Last, but certainly not least, my sincere thanks goes to Red Schoendienst, Germantown's favorite son. Thank you for reminding us how the values we grow up with in a small town can influence our lives.

All photographs are courtesy of the author's collection unless otherwise indicated.

INTRODUCTION

"Dear brothers and sisters, / It is nearly a year that I said goodbye to you and arrived in America." Thus begins a series of letters by Theodore Thole, a German immigrant, who settled in Hanover (now called Germantown). He wrote his first letter in 1854.

"Hanover is a little town 12 hours from St. Louis and 7 hours from the Okaw [River] and Vertsville [now Fayetteville] . . . There are many German Catholics living here, and this summer here in Hanover, a new church was built . . . I wouldn't advise anyone to come, for many don't like it in America the first time. Those who come must learn everything because work here is quite different from Germany. Those who like traveling and know that they will be farmhands for their whole lives in Germany can have a much better life here."

Germantown is the oldest town in Clinton County. The German immigrants who came to Illinois first settled in this area. The village of Hanover formed around the desire to provide Catholic worship services for a small settlement of German families on Shoal Creek.

Records indicate that pioneers settled in the area of Shoal Creek and Germantown as early as 1816. A settlement began to develop in 1833, and the settlers bought 120 acres of what was called "church land" from an American named L. White in 1837. The settlers divided the land and sold tracts to pay for it.

In his *Record of the Catholic Settlement of Clinton County, Illinois*, Fr. Bartholomew Bartles comments, "It is strange that in all the settlements of Catholic Low Germans known to us here . . . the settlers coming via and from St. Louis passed over land far richer and closer to the market to settle in the swampy, fever-infested sections, where many, especially during the first years, succumbed to malaria."

The German immigrants sought out land with creeks and timber. They formerly owned farmland in Europe in the valleys of the Ems and Rhine Rivers. The land around Shoal Creek resembled their native land. The Germans had experience with draining the land and skillful tilling, thus creating the fertile farmland the township enjoys today.

These first homesteaders had an abiding faith in God and a willingness to make sacrifices for what they believed. Stories of the hardships they faced and conquered are beyond words. Their will to survive and stay in this land are inspiring. There are stories of a prairie fire in which a mother and child burned to death while in flight to a neighboring farmhouse. There are stories of the epidemics: two of Elizabeth Sandman's sons died of an illness that had them covered with black spots. Her neighbors left two coffins outside her door. She had to place the boys in the coffins and close the door. She was never able to find out where her sons were buried. Gerhard Gesenhues lost four of his seven children and his wife to illness. During the epidemics, people knew when a man, woman, or child died in the village by the sound of the tolling church bells. Everyone was afraid. During the flu epidemic, a funeral service would be held outside with the immediate family in front of the doors of the church. There are stories of daily hardships: Mary Eversgerd burned to death in her home because coal oil splashed on her dress when she was near the stove. While working in a field, a young man and his horses were struck by lightning.

In the beginning, worship services were held in a small house with no benches or chairs. A split-oak log on four props served as the communion rail. In 1840, a log church was built.

As the story goes, some wanted to call the settlement Westphalia, and some wanted to call it Hanover, as many of the settlers came from these areas in Germany. The name Hanover-Westphalia was even proposed. An argument ensued. Finally, someone got up and with a piece of chalk wrote the name Hanover above the door. And so the name Hanover was chosen. Later, when the town had its own post office, the name of the town had to be changed because there was another town in Illinois called Hanover, and this caused confusion with the mail. The town's name was changed to Germantown in honor of its German forefathers.

The spirit of sacrifice and the settlers' devotion to their religion is again revealed in the building of the present stone church. Not only did they assume the debt, but they also performed arduous personal services for a long period. It was very difficult for the settlers to pay their pledges to the church. One farmer even sold his team of oxen to pay his share of the debt. The same devotion to their church is revealed in the provisions of some wills. Frank Vogelsang included in his will in 1864, "to St. Henricus church in Hanover, Clinton County, Illinois, $100 for a new tower." And in his will, Peter Stammen stated that his daughter Josephine must give $500 to the church before she can inherit his farm. The church was originally called St. Henricus Catholic Church, but in 1867, the church was placed under the patronage of Saint Boniface, the patron saint of Germany.

Today, the people of Germantown remember and honor their German ancestors in many ways. The town's logo has an illustration of three linden tree leaves. Linden trees were brought from Germany and planted in the churchyard. They represent the enduring faith and strength of the settlement and continue to be planted in the churchyard even today. Germantown keeps an Old World atmosphere through its architecture and main streetscape. Old traditions—such as the St. Boniface Catholic Church picnic, Sunday afternoon dances at the American Legion Hall, and Saturday night bingo—add to the town's character. The annual Spassfest celebrates Germantown's past and helps to build the community's future.

Germantown's history and rich German heritage cannot be exhausted through the confines of a single book. Instead, it must be a compilation of many perspectives. Only then can we realize the sacrifices, hardships, joys, and triumphs of our ancestors and appreciate their legacy.

Germantown is the oldest town in Clinton County. It was originally called Hanover because many of the German settlers came from the Kingdom of Hanover in Germany. This aerial view, taken in 1983, shows that St. Boniface Catholic Church is at the center of the community. The village is full of German history, traditions, and customs, some of which continue today. But more importantly, the character of Germantown is in its people and their strong sense of community. (Courtesy of Tom Lampe.)

One

A CATHOLIC SETTLEMENT

The early churches of the settlement were dedicated to Saint Henry. In 1867, the present church was placed under the patronage of Saint Boniface. This scene is on the wall of the sanctuary behind the altar. Saint Boniface was a missionary in Germany. The story of Saint Boniface says he cut down a large oak tree that was dedicated to Jupiter and used the wood to build a church. (Photograph by Patrick Lampe; courtesy of Tom Lampe.)

The Kickapoo and Illinois Indians hunted in this area. They lived in small villages and had a peaceful life. The German immigrants, more than any other group of settlers, got along well with the Indians. These Native American artifacts are displayed at Bob Eversgerd's Fort. This Civil War fort and museum is located on Old Shoal Creek Road, two miles south of State Route 161. (Courtesy of Bob Eversgerd.)

Immigrants who came to America in the 1800s carried their belongings in plain wooden trunks. This immigrant box belonged to Gerhardt Langenhorst, whose name is inscribed on the trunk. A journey on a sailing ship sometimes lasted for months. Food became rancid and drinking water was brackish. Conditions were crowded and unsanitary, and many died of starvation or disease. (Courtesy of Joe Langenhorst.)

Gerhardt Langenhorst and his family came to America in 1856. Members of the Langenhorst family in this photograph are, from left to right, (first row) Herman, Gerhardt, Frank, Margaretha (Peters), and Annie; (second row) Henry, Ben, and Josephine. This photograph was taken by John Strathmann soon after the Langenhorsts arrived. Strathmann had a photography studio in Germantown. (Courtesy of Joe Langenhorst.)

Herman Joseph Niebur was born in Lengerich, Westphalia, Germany. He came to America in 1852. His original family farm is located west of Germantown on State Route 161 at Hunter Road. He married Mary Elizabeth Stolte and built a house on the southwest corner of Sycamore and Locust Streets in 1888. It later became the Joseph Jansen home.

Gerhard Gesenhues emigrated from Epe, Westphalia, Germany, in 1858. He moved to Hanover where he owned property between Prairie and Munster Streets. He was married twice but lost both of his wives. This photograph was taken in 1896 and shows Gerhard with daughters Rose (left) and Frances. He was a cooper and the treasurer for the Hanover Star Milling Company. Frances married Joseph Jansen, who began the Jansen Chevrolet Company.

Bernard Husmann emigrated from Germany with his family in the mid-1840s. Like many, Bernard came to America as a small child. His parents were farmers. He later married Anne Schulte, another German immigrant. They were the ancestors of Elmer Husmann, a well-known businessman who repaired saddles, sold sewing machines, and made and repaired shoes. Elmer's shop was on Main Street. (Courtesy of Pat Frerker.)

The Germans who immigrated to this area were the first Germans to settle in the state of Illinois. They became the founders and pillars of Germantown. Shown at right, John and Catherine Welling were two of these people. John T. Welling came here from Gelderland, Holland, in 1853. He was only about two years old. His father was a tailor. Welling's hardware store is a landmark, and the building still stands on the corner of Main and Prairie Streets. Shown below, during the latter part of the 19th century and early part of the 20th century, the entire block between Main and Church Streets housed several factories owned by J.T. Welling. He owned a furniture store, a tin shop, and a sawmill. He made furniture and coffins, and an undertaker worked in the back of his store. (Both courtesy of John and Florence Duncan.)

Herman and Christine Robben lived in the brick house that still stands on the corner of Walnut and Prairie Streets. They owned and operated Robben's General Store, which was located on the corner of Munster and Walnut Streets. One resident recalls that in the early 1900s, Robben's store sold bananas for a nickel each. Customers could break a banana right off of a large banana cluster. (Courtesy of Carolyn Santel.)

Germantown is the first true German settlement in Illinois. Immigrants came here as early as 1833. As part of the centennial celebration on October 8, 1933, residents rode through the streets in spring wagons depicting the arrival of the early settlers. Some people who took part in the reenactment were Joseph Lampe (dressed as an Indian), Gus Heidemann (dressed as an early settler), Anna Frerker, and Pete Meier (both on wagon). (Courtesy of Sue Kalmer.)

16

St. Boniface Catholic Church was completed in 1854. The church faces Munster Street and is situated in the middle of the town. This illustration may have been an artist's rendition of the church, the rectory, and the old brick school. It includes inserts of the convent and the teacher's residence. The drawing was found in 1953 inside an upstairs wall of Brockmann's Store on Main Street.

A large brick school south of the church was built in 1893. It often served as a Catholic hall for various events. As the community grew, a gymnasium and additional classrooms were built. It was demolished in 1967, but the memory of the school evokes recollections of penny socials, the merry-go-round by the convent, and days when a handbell signaled the end of recess. (Courtesy of Tom Lampe.)

On October 13, 1924, the boys who attended the one-room schoolhouse known as the "Big Boys School" posed for this picture. The school was located on the corner of Walnut and Westfall Streets. The boys were constantly playing tricks on their teacher, Mr. Gramann, so they could get out of school early. During recess in the winter, the boys threw snowballs into the attic. When the snowballs melted and dripped down into the classroom, the teacher thought the roof was leaking and sent the boys home early. They also rigged a fine wire to the hands of the school's clock in the back of the classroom. When the teacher's head was turned toward the blackboard, one boy tugged on the wire to move the hands of the clock forward. One day, the boy tugged too hard, the hands of the clock broke, and Mr. Gramann (known as "Teacher Gramann") found out the scheme. (Courtesy of Edna Lakenburges.)

These are proud eighth-grade graduates from the class of 1957. This photograph also shows the interior of the old school. The graduates are posed in the gymnasium and the balcony is in the background. Generations of children attended this school and can remember creaky stairways with large wooden banisters, homemade lunches in the cafeteria, and janitor "Hermie" Schniers. (Courtesy of Dorothy Holtmann.)

This bus driver delivered generations of children to and from school in Germantown. Gerald Jansen began driving a bus in 1937 when he was 17 years old. He drove his classmates to Aviston High School and drove workers to the shoe factory in Carlyle. Later, he became the first school bus contractor for Germantown Elementary School. He drove the bus for 50 years without an accident and retired in 1988.

Sister Eurose and her first-grade class of 1954 are standing next to the church for this photograph. From left to right are the following: (first row) Sister Eurose, Ted Haar, Marvin Roettering, Leo Albers, Elaine Wildhaber, Carol Thuenemann, Janet Dierkes, Betty Hemann, Ray Haake, and David "Jeff" Timmermann; (second row) Ron Mollet, Marvin Warnecke, David Schlautmann, Ron Huegen, Louella Robke, Pat Husmann, August Heidemann, Edward Olliges, Glennon Backman, and Walter "Skip" Diesen. (Courtesy of Maurice Dierkes.)

In 1967, under the direction of Fr. John Boomkens, the new elementary school complex was built on the southeast corner of the church property. The original building included 12 classrooms, a kitchen and lunchroom facilities, and a large gymnasium. Due to increased enrollment, two additional temporary classrooms facing Westfall Street were purchased in 1970. Later, a new wing was constructed with additional classrooms, thus creating a junior high school.

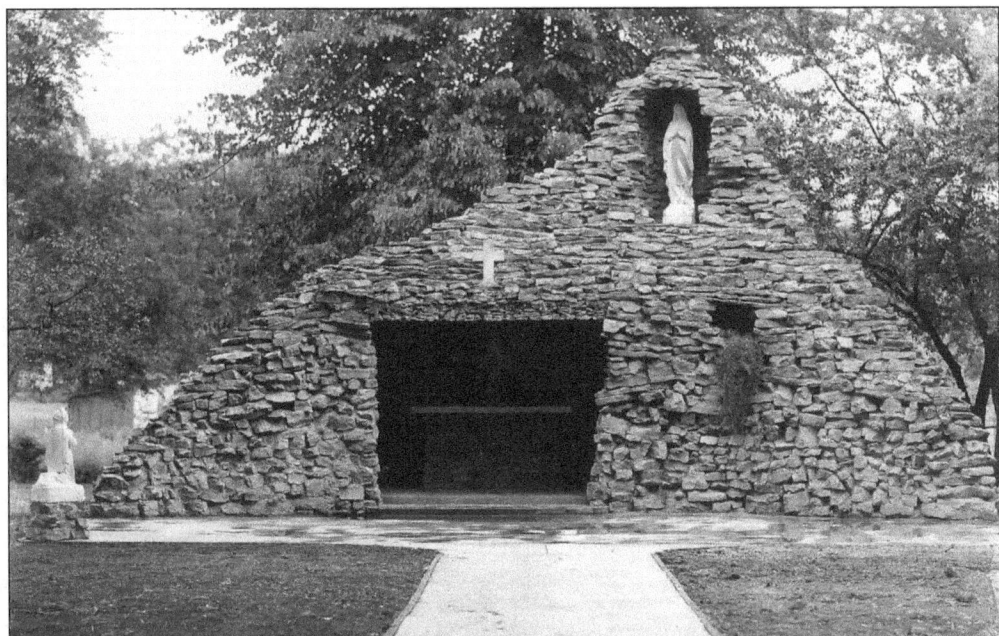

Another example of the town's German influence is the Our Lady of Lourdes grotto. *Grot* is the Dutch word for cave. It was built next to the rectory and dedicated by Bishop Albert R. Zuroweste on May 22, 1952. The grotto was built because the parish priest and parents feared that the young people at the parish were being exposed to many spiritual dangers and needed the protection of the Blessed Mother. (Courtesy of Joe Langenhorst.)

The St. Boniface convent was built in 1870. It was located on the south side of the church. The Poor Handmaids of Jesus Christ taught in the school until 1975 and played a significant role in the care and religious education of the community. This is a photograph of the altar in the convent. It was handcrafted by August Lampe Sr. (Courtesy of Regis and Barb Voss.)

Die sechs nothwendigen Glaubensstücke.

1. Es ist nur ein Gott, der alles erschaffen hat, erhält und regiert.
2. Gott ist ein gerechter Richter; er belohnt das Gute und bestraft das Böse.
3. In der Gottheit sind drei Personen: Vater, Sohn und Heiliger Geist.
4. Die zweite Person in der Gottheit ist Mensch geworden, um uns durch seinen Tod zu erlösen und selig zu machen.
5. Die Seele des Menschen ist unsterblich.
6. Die Gnade Gottes ist zur Seligkeit nothwendig.

Die zehn Gebote Gottes.

1. Ich bin der Herr, dein Gott. Du sollst keine fremden Götter neben mir haben; du sollst dir kein geschnitztes Bild machen, dasselbe anzubeten.
2. Du sollst den Namen Gottes, deines Herrn, nicht eitel nennen.
3. Gedenke, daß du den Sabbat heiligest.
4. Du sollst Vater und Mutter ehren, auf daß es dir wohl gehe und du lange lebest auf Erden.
5. Du sollst nicht tödten.
6. Du sollst nicht ehebrechen.
7. Du sollst nicht stehlen.
8. Du sollst nicht falsches Zeugniß geben wider deinen Nächsten.
9. Du sollst nicht begehren deines Nächsten Weib.
10. Du sollst nicht begehren deines Nächsten Haus, Acker, Knecht, Magd, Ochs, Esel, noch alles was sein ist.

Die Gebote der Kirche.

1. Du sollst an Sonn- und Feiertagen die heilige Messe hören.
2. Du sollst die Fast- und Abstinenztage halten.
3. Du sollst wenigstens einmal im Jahre beichten und in der Osterzeit communiciren.
4. Du sollst dich keiner verbotenen Gesellschaft anschließen.

Six Truths which we must know and believe.

1. There is only *one* God who created all things, and who preserves and governs all things.
2. God is a just Judge, who rewards the good and punishes the wicked.
3. In God there are three Persons: the Father, the Son and the Holy Ghost.
4. The second Person of the Blessed Trinity became man, to redeem us by His death and to make us eternally happy.
5. The soul is immortal.
6. The grace of God is necessary for salvation.

The Ten Commandments of God.

1. I am the Lord thy God. Thou shalt not have strange gods before me; thou shalt not make to thyself any graven thing to adore it.
2. Thou shalt not take the name of the Lord thy God in vain.
3. Remember that thou keep holy the Sabbath day.
4. Honor thy father and thy mother, that it may be well with thee, and thou mayest live long on the earth.
5. Thou shalt not kill.
6. Thou shalt not commit adultery.
7. Thou shalt not steal.
8. Thou shalt not bear false witness against thy neighbor.
9. Thou shalt not covet thy neighbor's wife.
10. Thou shalt not covet thy neighbor's house, nor his field, nor his servant, nor his handmaid, nor his ox, nor his ass, nor anything that is his.

The Commandments of the Church.

1. To hear Mass on Sundays and Holydays of obligation.
2. To fast and to abstain on the days appointed.
3. To confess at least once a year and to receive Holy Communion at Easter or within the time appointed.
4. Not to join forbidden societies.

Many remember studying the *Baltimore Catechism*. Students were required to memorize the answers to the questions as part of their religious education. The pages shown here are from *Catechism for the Catholic Parochial Schools in the United States*. The book was published in 1916 and owned by Josephine Welling. It contains both German and English. The pages mirror each other, with the German text on the left page and the English text on the right page. On one of the pages shown here, the tenth commandment states, "Thou shalt not covet thy neighbor's house, nor his field, nor his servant, nor his handmaid, nor his ox, nor his ass, nor anything that is his." It also lists six truths that Catholics must believe and several commandments of the church. (Courtesy of Dave Lampe.)

The beautiful stained glass windows at St. Boniface Catholic Church were installed in the 1890s. Many were given in memory of the early residents of Germantown. These windows are etched with a dedication written in German. This particular window depicts Saint Elizabeth. It was given in memory of Gerhard and Mary Elizabeth (Stolte) Gesenhues.

Many families had children who entered the religious life. The parish priest was a mentor for the seminarians. In this photograph from 1950, Fr. John Boomkens is standing outside St. Boniface Catholic Church with four local seminarians. They are, from left to right, James Jansen, unidentified, Father Boomkens, Floyd Boeckmann, and Charles Boeckmann.

JESUS NIMMT DAS
KREUZ AUF SICH

The St. Boniface Cemetery is located on the corner of Sycamore and Munster Streets. The first cemetery was located directly north of the present church but was moved during the cholera plague of the 1850s. Pictured above is a recent photograph of the crucifixion group carved from marble. It was cited as a Clinton County landmark in 1986. Shown at left, the cemetery is known for the beautiful Stations of the Cross that line the road through the cemetery. The stations came from Rome and were a gift from the Casper and Katherine Stroot family in the 1800s. Each scene had to be transported by horse-drawn wagon from the railroad depot. Each is encased in a concrete pillar and displayed behind glass. The inscription below each one is in German. This is the second station and reads, "Jesus shoulders the cross."

This funeral card is further evidence of the German presence in Germantown. These cards were a memorial and had a religious picture on the opposite side. This particular card is from 1887 and is a remembrance from the funeral of Maria Franzista Gesenhues. She was 23 years old when she died.

"Darum wachet, denn ihr wisset nicht, zu welcher Stunde euer Herr kommen wird." Matth. XXIV, 42.

"Wer den Herrn fürchtet, dem wird's wohl gehen an seinem Ende, der wird gesegnet werden am Tage seines Hinscheidens." Ecclus. I, 14.

"Der Herr hat's gegeben, der Herr hat's genommen. Wie es dem Herrn gefallen hat, also ist's geschehen! Der Name des Herrn sei gebenedeit." Job, I, 21.

✝

Zum frommen Andenken

—an—

Maria Franziska Gesenhues,

geboren zu Germantown, Clinton Co., Ills., am 27. Juli 1864, gestorben am Mittwoch Nachmittag, den 20. April, 1887, ebendaselbst.

Wir bitten die Gläubigen, für die liebe Verstorbene zu beten, damit der barmherzige Gott ihr die ewige Ruhe verleihe. **Laßt uns beten.**

Verzeih', barmherziger Vater, deiner Dienerin Maria Franziska, was sie aus menschlicher Schwachheit gefehlt hat. Vergib ihr, wenn sie etwa noch nicht ganz rein von Fehlern vor deinem Richterstuhle erschienen ist, Um unseres Gebetes willen kürze ab die Zeit der Läuterung, führe sie bald zum Reiche der Seligen zur ewigen Herrlichkeit. Durch Jesum Christum, unsern Herrn. Amen!

Vater unser. Gegrüßet seist du Maria.

There is a cross that greets parishioners as they come up the sidewalk to St. Boniface Catholic Church. The monument is inscribed with several dates. Each year indicates a time when the church held a three-day mission or service. It is further evidence that Germantown has always had a firm foundation in the church. (Photograph by Patrick Lampe; courtesy of Tom Lampe.)

25

These girls participated in a May Day procession at St. Boniface Church. May Day was a celebration of the Blessed Virgin Mary. The photograph, taken in the 1930s, shows, from left to right, Dorothy (Winter) Beckmann, unidentified, Helen (Maue) Brand, and Marcella Robben. (Courtesy of Pat Reed and Helen Brand.)

Many classes from Germantown Elementary School had their graduation photographs taken in front of the Our Lady of Lourdes grotto. This is the class of 1971. The two teachers standing on each end of this group of students are Neil Welz (left) and Tom Lampe. (Courtesy of Dorothy Holtmann.)

These people posed for this photograph on the 50th wedding anniversary of John Henry and Mary Elizabeth (Weier) Budde in 1924. Both German immigrants, John was born in Banvinkle, and Mary was born in Thuene. John is seated in front on the left, and Mary is beside him. The woman seated next to Mary is her sister. John and Mary's house was located in Germantown on the corner of Church and Locust Streets. (Courtesy of the Christine Budde family.)

These children are outside of the old school and posing for a photograph taken on October 13, 1924. Three sisters from the Joseph Jansen family are in this group. Mary Ann Jansen is the third from right on the second row. Marcella (Jansen) Nagel is the fifth from right on the fourth row. Dolores Jansen, who later became Sr. Dolores Marie, is on the right end of the seventh row.

On the 25th wedding anniversary of Herman and Christine Robben, the family posed for this photograph. It was taken in 1912. From left to right appear the following family members: (first row) Henry, mother Christine, father Herman Sr., and Herman Jr.; (second row) Elizabeth (Schoendienst), Mamie (Schoendienst), Lena (Maue), and George. (Courtesy of Carolyn Santel.)

St. Boniface Catholic Church has many stained glass windows to add to its beauty. The windows were renovated in 2002. During that time, one of the windows was stolen in a truck theft. A police search ensued, and the window was found about a week later. The thieves had wrapped the delicate sections of the antique church window. (Photograph by Patrick Lampe; courtesy of Tom Lampe.)

The four bells in the church tower at St. Boniface Catholic Church testify to the faith of Germantown's ancestors. They each bear the name of a saint. The bells are known as Saint Cecilia, Saint Joseph, Saint Maria, and Saint Henricus. One of the German inscriptions on the Saint Cecilia bell reads, "Sing to God Forever." Fr. John Boomkens required that the church bells ring the Angelus Prayer at five o'clock every evening. (Photograph by Patrick Lampe; courtesy of Tom Lampe.)

A photograph taken of the interior of St. Boniface Catholic Church in the early 1900s shows the high altar that was once in the sanctuary. On the left side is an elevated pulpit. It was decorated with golden images of the four gospel writers, Matthew, Mark, Luke, and John. This pulpit was replaced by a wooden pulpit that stands on the floor of the sanctuary. (Courtesy of Regis and Barb Voss.)

Above is a photograph of the rectory that was constructed in 1870. It was replaced by a new rectory in 1975. To date, 29 priests have been assigned to St. Boniface parish. Fr. James Buerster is the current pastor. Shown below, the Poor Handmaids of Jesus Christ, an order of nuns, played an important part in the history of Germantown. This photograph shows the convent. The nuns served as nurses in the early history of the parish and as teachers in the schools for 100 years. They had a profound effect upon the education and spiritual life of the town. Hosts were made by the sisters upstairs in the convent and used for Eucharistic celebrations. Just as some of the young men from St. Boniface parish entered the priesthood and were mentored by the parish priest, some of the young women became nuns and received care and guidance from the sisters. (Both courtesy of Tom Lampe.)

Two

TOWN AND COUNTRY

This map of the original town of Germantown is from the 1892 Standard Atlas of Clinton County. The first Germans who settled in Clinton County located in this area. Germantown Township includes the village plus unincorporated and rural areas. The township is situated in the southern part of the county and is bounded by Breese Township on the north, Washington County on the south, Santa Fe Township on the east, and Looking Glass Township on the west. (Courtesy of Joe Langenhorst).

The main street through Germantown was Munster Street. This is a photograph of Munster Street as it was in the 1800s. These people have taken a moment to pose for a traveling photographer. The cross street is Walnut Street. The white house on the left is still standing today. (Courtesy of Pat Reed.)

This beer delivery wagon is outside one of the oldest buildings in Germantown. Made of native lumber and wooden pegs instead of nails, this tavern still stands on Main Street and was the location of the first village meetings. It also served as a place to vote. People prepared their ballots outside and brought them to a window of the building where they were given to an official counter. (Courtesy of Pat Reed.)

Robben's General Store was one of the oldest stores in town. Herman and Christine Robben established the store in the 1800s. Until the early 1960s, the store was located at the corner of Munster and Walnut Streets. A dentist named Dr. Hardy came from New Baden once a week. He saw patients in a dental chair upstairs. At that time, dentists did not use anesthetics. (Courtesy of Carolyn Santel.)

This picture was taken in 1958. It is an aerial view of south Munster Street. The house on the left side of the street is still standing and was once Dr. Bernard Mierink's home and doctor's office. Farther south and across Walnut Street was Robben's General Store. (Courtesy of Connie Kampwerth.)

Herman and Christine Robben's son Henry had a jewelry shop that was attached to Robben's General Store. This photograph was taken between 1900 and 1911 in front of the jewelry shop. In the carriage, from left to right, are Mamie Schoendienst, Lena Maue, and George Robben. Standing on the ground are Herman Robben and Lizzie Schoendienst. Henry established the jewelry store on the east side of the street in 1909. Shown below is a photograph of Henry inside his store. After Henry's wife passed away, he married Lizzie Niemeyer. They established the Robben & Niemeyer clothing store in the neighboring town of Breese. (Both courtesy of Pat Reed and Helen Brand.)

At right, Henry Schurmann was another early businessman who helped develop Germantown in the 1800s. His father, Peter Schurmann, came here from Westphalia, Germany. Henry began working for the Hanover Star Milling Company when he was 12 years old. The photograph below shows the Hanover Star Milling Company in the 1900s. It is still located on Market Street. In 1889, Henry Schurmann obtained the right-of-way for the Southern Railroad to come through Germantown. He purchased much of the right-of-way himself to have railroad facilities for the mill. Railroad cars were diverted from the main track and taken into the mill to be loaded with flour and grain. (Right, courtesy of Ethan Deerhaake; below, courtesy of Tom Lampe.)

In the 1800s, there was a cooper shop behind the Hanover Star Milling Company. A cooper was someone who made barrels. The photograph above shows some of the early employees of the cooper shop. Herman Beckmann is third from the left. Below is a photograph that shows the process. The coopers would roll their finished products across a steel bridge that led from the cooper shop over the millpond to the mill. The barrels were then pushed through a window so they could be packed with flour. (Above, courtesy of Pat Frerker; below, courtesy of Tom Lampe.)

The Southern Railroad came through Germantown in 1889. The railroad company planned to run the tracks south of Germantown, but Henry Schurmann obtained the right-of-way for the railroad to run along Clinton Street. The railroad transported flour and grain from the Hanover Star Milling Company, brought visitors to the town, exported dairy products from the creamery, and delivered mail. (Courtesy of Tom Lampe.)

The railroad was important for the town's commerce and had to be maintained. When work was being done on the track, a railcar was used for transporting people and equipment. This photograph was taken in the early 1900s, and these workers have stopped shoveling for a moment to pose. (Courtesy of Joe Langenhorst.)

Almost every house had a picket fence. Families were large and the fences protected their children. This photograph is from the 1800s and shows the Schniers home on the northwest corner of Sycamore and Locust Streets. However, in this picture there is no Locust Street yet. The house still stands and is one of the town's older homes. (Courtesy of Joe Langenhorst.)

A street scene taken in the 1920s shows several businesses on Munster Street. Dr. B.J. Meierink's house is on the left side of the street. Theodore "Toby" Hoff's house, his shoe store, and the Fruth Brothers' Garage are seen on the right side of the street. The man in the foreground is roping off the street for an event.

Above is a photograph of Schlarmann's slaughterhouse. It was located on the northeast corner of Walnut and Elm Streets. In the 1800s and early 1900s, people depended on farmers to deliver milk and eggs. Meat was slaughtered locally and delivered to stores. At right is a photograph of T.W. Schlarmann. Known as "Butcher Bill," Schlarmann was Germantown's famous blind butcher. Schlarmann's Market was located on Munster Street between the IGA grocery store and the post office. Starting in the mid-1930s, Schlarmann's eyesight began to fail. He became almost completely blind, but stayed in business. He taught himself the exact location of every item on the shelves. In those days, the store clerk retrieved customers' groceries. He also taught himself how to cut meat by feel. (Above, courtesy of Irene Schoendienst; right, courtesy of Sr. Genevieve Schlarmann.)

One of the oldest and most familiar businesses in Germantown is the IGA grocery on Munster Street directly across from the St. Boniface Catholic Church. It was built in 1853 and was originally owned by Ben Eversgerd. At one time, it was a hotel. After Eversgerd became sick, his brother Hank bought the store and partnered with Jack Albers. The original store building was demolished in 1955; the new store built in its place still operates today. (Courtesy of Shirley Eversgerd.)

The grand opening of Hank Eversgerd's new store was in 1956. He made the century stone on the front of the store. The school lunches, food for the taverns and restaurants in town, and even the "funeral hotdogs" come from the IGA store. It is part of the town's character and is a landmark. (Courtesy of Shirley Eversgerd.)

Welling's Hardware and Manufacturing Company was established in 1874. It was one of the oldest businesses in Clinton County and began three years after Germantown was organized as a village. A fire in 1910 destroyed the store. It was rebuilt without the living quarters that were on the second floor of the original store. (Courtesy of John and Florence Duncan.)

Albin and Josephine Husmann lived on Locust Street. The Sandal-Craft Shoe Factory can be seen in the background. These three young ladies have stopped to pose for a photograph in the Husmanns' yard. They are, from left to right, Clara Albers, Josephine (Beckmann) Husmann, and Sarah Linnemann. The photograph was taken in the mid-1940s. (Courtesy of Pat Frerker.)

Elmer Husmann started his business in 1932 as a shoe and harness repair shop. He also repaired buggy seats and made harness sets. The small shop in this photograph was located behind his house on Main Street. Later, he had a larger repair shop built next to his home. (Courtesy of Derrick Husmann.)

Husmann's shoe repair shop was on Main Street. Elmer Husmann built the shop shown in this photograph in 1954. He repaired and sold shoes and sewing machines. Husmann was quite handy and could repair anything from a washing machine to an old pair of shoes. The building was torn down in 2008. (Courtesy of Carolyn Beer.)

42

The present Cornerstone Bar and Grill began as the Arcade Saloon in 1907. It was owned by Henry Bohnkemper and later by his son Fred. In 1963, Vince Wessling rented the tavern, and he later bought it. Then it was commonly known as Vince's Corner Tavern. After his death, daughters Diane and Joyce, with their mother, Eleanor, changed the name to Cornerstone Bar and Grill. (Courtesy of Loretta Frey.)

On May 10, 2003, Cornerstone Bar and Grill celebrated its 40th anniversary. Pictured here are the members of the Cornerstone family. The boy in front is Jason Kuhl. Others are, from left to right, as follows: (first row) Charlene (Wessling) Albers, T.M. Albers, Joyce (Wessling) Kuhl, Jennifer (Schniers) Huegen, Julie (Schniers) Musenbrock, and Diane (Wessling) Schniers; (second row) Scott Albers, Mark Albers, Diane (Beckmann) Kuhl, Dan Musenbrock, and Stan Schniers; (third row) Dennis "Boomer" Kuhl, Doug Kuhl, and John Schniers. (Courtesy of Diane and Stanley Schniers.)

Local taverns have always been gathering places. In the photograph above from 1969, members of a local bowling team met at Vince's Tavern to have a beer or two after the game. From left to right are the following: (first row) Vince Wessling (the owner) and Greg "Do" Albers; (second row) Ray Beckmann, Alfred Mensing, Art Lubers, Paul Jansen, and Erv Winkler. In the photograph below, the wives have come to Vince's as well. They are shown from left to right as follows: Jane Lubers, Marge Jansen, Eleanor Wessling, Florence Beckmann, Evie Mensing, and Rose Winkler. (Both courtesy of Diane and Stanley Schniers.)

Joseph "Joe" Micheel started cutting hair in the early 1900s when he was 15. He worked with another barber named Mr. Coony in this little shop on Munster Street. Micheel is standing outside the shop. He later moved to Main Street and continued the business on his own. (Courtesy of Connie Kampwerth.)

Located on Main Street, the house in this photograph was built by Herman Schlueter in 1883 as a watchmaker's shop. Over the years, it also served as a post office, millinery shop, and hotel. In the early 1900s, Joe Micheel and his wife, Elizabeth, moved here and ran a barbershop for many years. (Courtesy of Virginia Kennett.)

This photograph of the Micheel family was taken in the 1940s. During the Great Depression, Joe Micheel wanted to ensure that his children would have a trade. Each of them went to school and became licensed barbers. His daughter Virginia became the first woman barber at Scott Air Force Base—a woman before her time—and later became a licensed beauty operator. The family is pictured from left to right as follows: (first row) Joe and Elizabeth; (second row), Roger, Lillian, Tom, Paul, Virginia, and Leon. (Courtesy of Virginia Kennett.)

Joseph Duncan was a salesman for the Hanover Star Milling Company and drove a delivery truck. On January 26, 1939, he attempted to stop his truck at a railroad crossing west of Germantown but slid into the path of an oncoming train. He was thrown from his vehicle and survived, but the train dragged the truck 1,200 feet. (Courtesy of John Duncan.)

Dr. Bernard John Meierink and his family lived in a small house on the northeast corner of Munster and Walnut Streets. Pictured here are members of his family. Shown from left to right are Bernard, Paul (son), Laura (daughter), and Frances Meierink (wife). This photograph was probably taken around 1900. (Courtesy of Connie Kampwerth.)

Germantown doctor Bernard John Meierink both lived in this house and saw patients here. He obtained his medical degree in 1899 and opened his practice in Germantown in 1900. Like several of the houses in Germantown, the Meierink residence is more than 100 years old. This picture was taken in 1963 and shows the old school in the background. (Courtesy of Connie Kampwerth.)

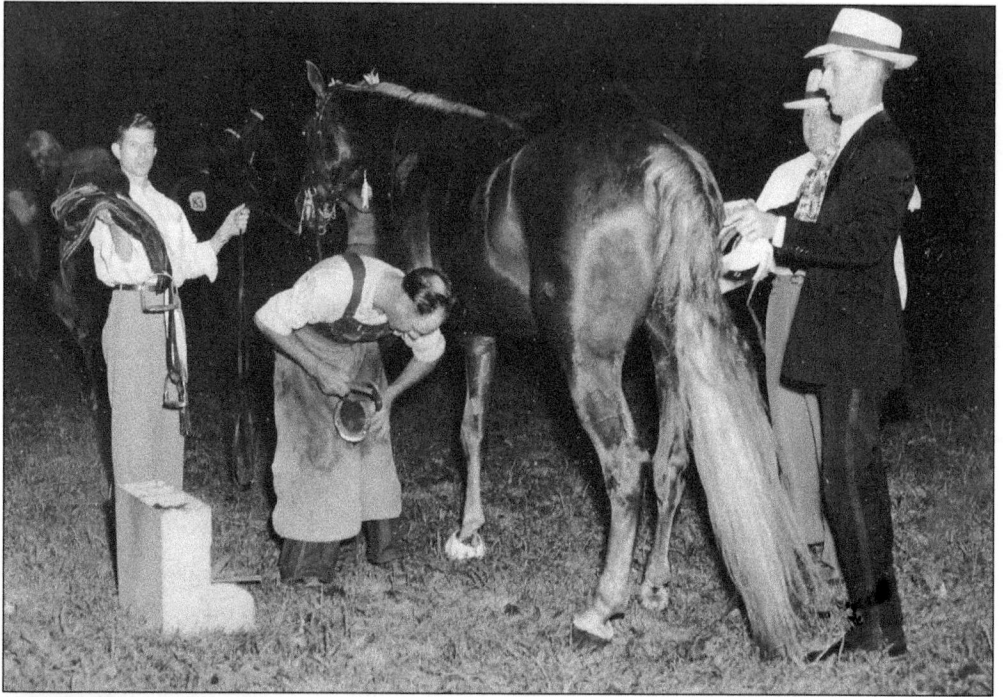

Blacksmith shops and car garages existed side-by-side. Even though some people had cars in the early 1900s, many people still used horses. Cars were expensive, and the town had dirt roads, which often had ruts and became muddy, making it difficult for cars to travel. The blacksmith bending over and shoeing the horse is Alphonse Lakenburges. The blacksmith shop was attached to Lakenburges Motor Company on Walnut Street. (Courtesy of Edna Lakenburges.)

Lakenburges Motor Company on the corner of Elm and Walnut Streets is another of the town's oldest businesses. The garage was established in 1898 by Henry Lakenburges. Upon his death, sons Alfonse and Jack took over the business. The business started as a blacksmith shop, then offered bicycle repair services and sold fencing and heavy hardware. Some of the early employees, from left to right, were John Lakenburges, Lukes Lakenburges, Mickey Schoendienst, and Joe "Seppo" Schoendienst. (Courtesy of Edna Lakenburges.)

This photograph from the 1920s shows Lukes Lakenburges standing on Elm Street next to the tow truck or "wrecker," as it was more commonly called. Lukes was the son of Henry Lakenburges and was Alfonse and Jack's brother. Four generations have worked at the Lakenburges Motor Company. Today, their main business is car repair, lawn mowers, and electric motors. (Courtesy of Edna Lakenburges.)

In 1952, Clarence "Stevie" Kohnen could not afford to buy culvert pipe for a ditch in front of his house, so he made his own. This photograph shows the homemade wheelbarrow he used that cost him $7 to make. He built it from an old wheel, a bed frame, and a metal panel from a car. It was the beginning of Kohnen Concrete Products, Inc. The plant is located on Green Street. (Courtesy of Clarence and Marcella Kohnen.)

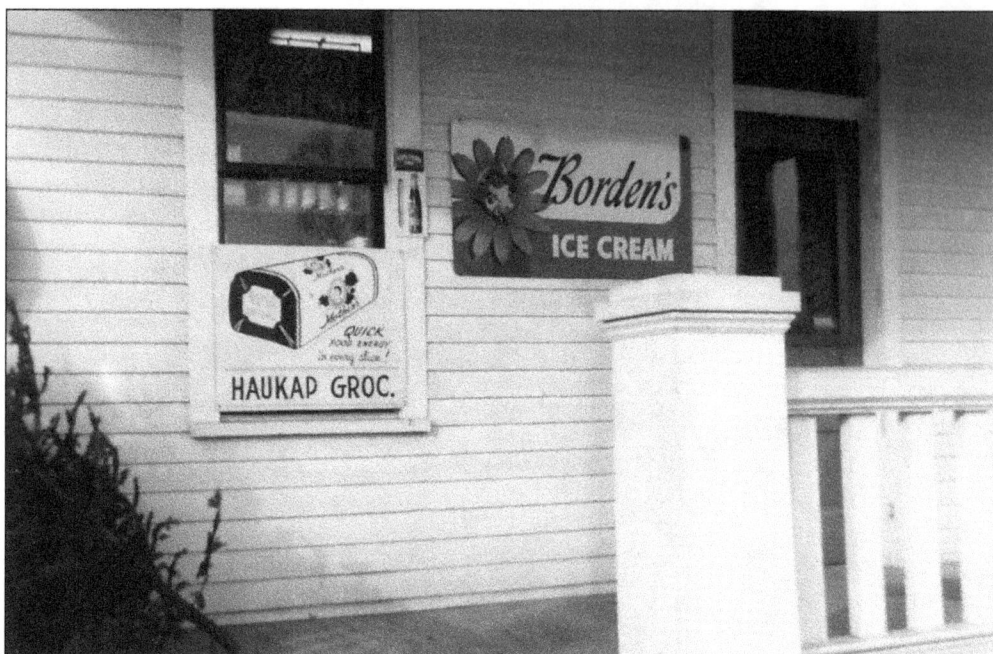

In the early 1950s, Minnie Haukap had a one-room grocery store in her home. It may have been the area's first convenience mart. Her little store was located on the northwest corner of Prairie and Walnut Streets. The store was discontinued in 1956, but the building still stands. Notice the tree on her front porch in the photograph above. Everyone had a real tree at Christmas, and they were usually purchased from the stores in town or chopped from the woods. The photograph below shows Minnie in her store. People entered the small store from the front porch. The selection was not large, but the store provided a living for the widow. (Both courtesy of Karen Rackers.)

After working on cars in an old livery stable, Joseph Jansen built the Jansen Chevrolet Company in 1926. This photograph shows the original workers, who appear from left to right as follows: Joseph Jansen, Fritz Robke, Ed Holtmann, Gerald Jansen, and Richard Jansen. A new Jansen Chevrolet dealership was built in 1968. It is located on the southeast corner of Sycamore and Munster Streets.

The Jansen boys are posing with the wrecker in this 1940s photograph. They are taking time out from their busy day of work at the garage. From left to right are Gerald, Jim, and Tom. Notice the telephone number on the truck. When telephone service came to Germantown, there were only three telephones in town. One of them was at Jansen Chevrolet Company. To be connected, the caller had to ask the operator for "number 2."

The old Germantown Savings Bank building is located on the northeast corner of Main and Market Streets. It was established in 1906, and the building still stands today. The original officers of the Germantown Savings Bank were president A.B. Daab and cashier H.H. Schlarmann. Originally, the people of Germantown deposited their savings at the local Hanover Star Milling Company. (Courtesy of James Lampe Sr.)

Members of the board of directors of the Germantown Savings Bank are shown in this photograph from 1942. They are, from left to right, John E. Michels; attorney Andrew O. Niehoff from Carlyle; president Peter P. Goetz from East St. Louis; cashier Henry C. Michels, assistant cashier Dorothy (Rosen) Humphrey, and Dr. Charles B. Michels. (Courtesy of James Lampe Sr.)

A photograph from the 1960s shows the inside of the bank that was on the corner of Main and Market Streets. Bank employees, from left to right, are James "Stix" Lampe, Ruth (Pille) Winkler, Kathy (Gebke) Bergman, Doris (Rhinehart) Meyer, and Mary "Pepe" (Leonard) Korte. The new bank on the corner of Munster and Main Streets opened on March 17, 1970. (Courtesy of James Lampe Sr.)

Germantown got its own Frostee-Freeze Freezette in 1952. This ice cream shop was originally owned by Louis Winter and was located on the northwest corner of Munster and Main Streets. Later, it was bought by Irvin Lampe and moved to a location on West Sycamore Street at State Route 161. (Courtesy of Rose Hemann.)

In 1963, Dr. Valerian Eversgerd, Joseph Heimann, and James Lampe bought controlling interest of the Germantown Savings Bank. These officers are pictured in the current bank on the corner of Main and Munster Streets. They include, from left to right, Dr. Valerian Eversgerd, H.J. "Hank" Eversgerd, Pete Meier, Joe Heimann, and James Lampe. (Courtesy of James Lampe Sr.)

The new Germantown Bank is on the corner of Main and Munster Streets. It replaced the old bank that was on the corner of Main and Market Streets. This new bank opened as Germantown Trust and Savings Bank in 1967. In 2009, it was ranked first in the state and one of the top 10 banks in the country.

Shown above, the Germantown Public Library opened in 1995. It is located on Munster Street between the IGA grocery store and the post office. Jack Bergmann died in 1992 and left a trust fund to build the library. At right is a photograph of Jack Bergmann taken in his youth. He liked to read and wanted to do something for the children of Germantown. After his death, the town was stunned to learn that he had set aside a substantial amount of money for a library. Bergmann specified that the money was to be held until after his brother's death, but brother Paul signed over his rights to three-fourths of the trust so it could be used immediately. The library continues to be an asset to the community. (Above, courtesy of the Germantown Public Library; right courtesy of Paul and Rena Bergmann.)

Above is a photograph of the lunch counter at the Starlite Restaurant in Germantown. Starlite was located west of town near the intersection of Route 161 and Sycamore Street. The picture was taken during the grand opening of the restaurant in 1958. Clarence "Stevie" Kohnen built the restaurant when he realized the town did not have a place to meet for a cup of coffee. Below, Starlite Restaurant became a landmark and part of the character of Germantown. A Laundromat was attached to the restaurant. Soon after opening the Starlite Restaurant, Kohnen built the Starlite Motel and Molitor's Filling Station. (Both courtesy of Clarence and Marcella Kohnen.)

Above is a photograph of the inside of J.T. Welling's hardware store in the early 1900s. The signs are advertising a 9¢ sale with items neatly organized and displayed. Below is a springtime display in the store window. At Christmastime, children loved looking at the toy displays in the windows. Many parents in town shopped at the store for Christmas gifts. Ann Heideman, a former employee, remembered that parents would bring their children to the store, and while the children chose the toys they wanted from Santa, the parents would quietly touch the item. That was how the sales clerks knew which toys the parents wanted to purchase. These pictures were probably taken in the 1920s. (Both courtesy of John and Florence Duncan.)

In 1892, John E. Michels began a grocery, meat market, and general merchandise store on the northeast corner of Main and Munster Streets. Son A.B. Michels took over the business after his father's death. He added a fresh meat department. Ignatz Beer was the first meat cutter. A dress shop was also operated in connection with the grocery store. (Courtesy of Tom Lampe.)

Walter and Olivia Brockmann bought the store from A.B. Michels. For many years, Walter operated a small market and his wife, Olivia, operated a dry goods department. The butcher was Nick Beer Sr. This is a picture of the Walter Brockmann family that was taken in 1960. From left to right are (first row) Sue, David, Olivia, and Walter; (second row) Ted and Fred. (Courtesy of Sue Meyers.)

58

Many Germantown residents remember Brockmann's store. This photograph was taken at the front of the store. The dry goods section was operated by Olivia Brockmann and is seen here as the back room on the left. Sue (Brockmann) Meyers's son John poses in front of a display of cigarettes. (Courtesy of Sue Meyers.)

When Brockmann's store was being torn down in 2010, an old diploma was found in a metal canister in the wall. The diploma belonged to Dr. Charles Joseph Gissy. It was from the Medical School in Philadelphia and was dated 1858. Gissy was an immigrant from France and is buried in St. Boniface Cemetery. (Photograph by Jeff Wuebbles.)

This Schrage family is out for a drive in a 1914 Ford Model T Touring Car. Henry and Catherine Schrage are seated in front. The girls in the back seat are, from left to right, Theresa, Anna, Catherine, and Lena. The boys standing next to the car are Theodore (left) and Edward. Ben is standing in the back of the car. (Courtesy of Stella Schoendienst Jeffries.)

TO OPEN
❶ PULL UP THIS FLAP
❷ CUT ON DOTTED LINE
❸ POUR
LIKE
THIS❸

5 LBS.

HANOVER
WHOLE WHEAT
GRAHAM FLOUR

MFD. BY
HANOVER STAR MILLING CO.
GERMANTOWN, ILLINOIS

From the mid-1800s into the 1900s, the Hanover Star Milling Company was widely known as a maker of select winter wheat flour and feed. The mill produced some of the finest flour in the country. Its special brands were Magnificent, advertised for delicious cakes; Rose High Paten and Star for easy bread making; and Wonder Flour for wonderful biscuits. Germantown stores stocked these flours in bags like the one shown. (Courtesy of Maurice Dierkes.)

The US Postal Service began delivering mail in Germantown on January 14, 1946. A photograph taken in 1952 shows the new post office, which replaced an old building on Munster Street. As in many small towns, the post office is still a gathering place where people get their mail and talk with friends. (Courtesy of Rosie Hemann.)

Munster Street was originally spelled "Muenster" for the city of Muenster, Germany. This photograph shows a view looking north on Munster Street in 1909. Shops and houses were built close to the street much like they were in villages in Germany. A state work crew covered this dirt street with concrete in 1935. (Courtesy of John Duncan.)

This photograph from 1948 shows the employees of the Sandal-Craft Shoe Factory in Germantown that was located at the corner of Main and Locust Streets. The employees are pictured from left to right as follows: (first row) Rosemary Haake, Agnes Warnecke, Esther Buenemeyer, Leona Albers, Rosie Albers, Loretta (Ripperda) Frey, Delores Robke, Delores Frerker, Marcella "Marcie" (Hemann) Robke, Marcella Nordhaus, Catherine Frerker, Helen Leonard, Florence Korte, and Loretta Schutte; (second row) Laura Albers, Esther Thuenemann, Dorothy Becker, Johanna Mensing, Eugenia

Ortmann, Virginia Ortmann, Delores Jansen, Bernice Diesen, Josephine Huegen, Blanche (Haake) Becker, Helen Netemeyer, Delores Haake, Loretta Hermeling, Henrietta (Spihlmann) Albers, and Dorothy Beckmann; (third row) Alvin Hilms, Alfred Rickhoff, Vincent Rickhoff, Paul Dierkes, Ben Budde, Elizabeth Hoff, unidentified, Emelia Heimann, Hilda Dierkes, Clara Rickhoff, unidentified, Leona Husmann, Evelyn Korte, Lucille Haake, Kate Hemann, Lorraine Hemann, Viola Pingsterhaus, Robert Hemann, Kenny Buenemeyer, and Cyril Schniers. (Courtesy of Loretta Frey.)

Brothers Herman and Ben Horstman came to the United States from Spahnhorrenstatte, Germany, in the mid-1800s. Herman married Elizabeth Tempe Sandman, and in 1881, they purchased a farm in Germantown. Their log home stood until 1976. The farm is still in the family and is owned by Regis and Barb Voss. The picture above was taken in the spring of 1975 and shows Regis and Barb's grandsons Mike (left) and Dan. At left is a photograph of the original family. From left to right are (first row) Mary (Horstman) Schomaker and Elizabeth (Tempe) Horstman; (second row) John Sandman, Herman Horstman, and Henry Horstman. The farm is 130 years old. (Both courtesy of Regis and Barb Voss.)

This is a photograph of a typical farm in Germantown in the early 1920s. At that time, Frank and Olivia Linnemann owned this farm, which was located on Wesclin Road. It was a dairy farm, and the cows were milked by hand. Many farms were small and had less than 100 acres of land because harvesting was also done by hand. (Courtesy of Pat Frerker.)

Threshing was a common practice on the farm at harvest time in 1926. The threshing machine, referred to as a "separator," divided the wheat grain from the husk, leaving just the straw shaft. These hard-working men stopped to pose for a photograph. From left to right are John Mueller, Ben Thuenemann, Tom Thuenemann, Albert Wellen, and Bud Mueller. (Courtesy of Edna Lakenburges.)

Bundles of wheat are being put through the threshing machine in this 1926 photograph. This separator was powered by a steam engine and did not move. The grain came out into a wagon while the straw was blown into a big haystack. (Courtesy of Edna Lakenburges.)

Threshing machines blew the straw shaft from the wheat into a huge stack. This photograph was taken in 1926 at threshing time. The two men shown in the picture used a ladder to climb to the top of this stack. The straw was often used in the barn for cattle. (Courtesy of Edna Lakenburges.)

Threshing wheat was hard work, but it was also an exciting time on the farm. Friends and neighbors came to help, so there were many visitors. In this photograph from 1940, the children are having fun riding in a box wagon. Pictured from left to right are (first row) Flavian Huegen, David Huegen, and Mildred Foppe; (second row) Florence Kuhn, Edna Mueller, Franklin Huegen, Lorene Foppe, and Joe Kuhn. (Courtesy of Edna Lakenburges.)

In the 1920s at harvest time, George Hermeling loaned out this threshing machine to farmers. At threshing time, neighbors knew to come and help. While the men worked in the fields, the women prepared a large meal for the farmhands that often included several kinds of meats and homemade pies. (Courtesy of Joe Langenhorst.)

Visitors were always welcome on the farm. The children in this photograph from 1940 are having fun on a cart ride. They are, from left to the right, (first row) Lorene Foppe, Edna Mueller, and Flavian Huegen; (second row) Virginia Mueller, Florence Kuhn, and unidentified (driver). (Courtesy of Edna Lakenburges.)

Farmers depended on crops for their livelihood. This photograph shows evidence of a drought in 1954. Temperatures climbed to more than 100 degrees Fahrenheit for 13 days in a row. The ground was dry with cracks that were deep enough to fit a person's finger up to the knuckle. (Courtesy of Joe Langenhorst.)

In November 2005, Germantown farmers had an exceptionally good corn harvest. There was so much corn that more storage was needed. The storage bins at the mill were filled beyond capacity, and some of the harvest had to be dumped on the ground. The excess corn was placed on a concrete slab at Kohnen Concrete Products on Green Street. (Courtesy of Carolyn Beer.)

There were several country schools in Germantown, including Woodlane, Merscher, and Wilken just to name a few. The Merscher School was located on the northeast corner of Munich and Pioneer Roads, where it still stands today. The school operated from the 1870s into the 1900s. In 1925, students from the school posed for this photograph with their teacher, Mary B. McQuade. (Courtesy of the Christine Budde family.)

Above is a photograph of the 1943 class at the Wilken School. This school was also known as the Bottom School. It was located a half-mile east of Shoal Creek Road. Country schools contained students from first grade through eighth grade, and if the class was large, this meant for some busy days. In July 1984, there was a Wilken School reunion for the class of 1943. Below, the following former students are, from left to right, (first row) Christine (Winkler) Budde, Evelyn (Korte) Pingsterhaus, Wilamine (Ripperda) Schroeder, and Leona (Pingsterhaus) Eversgerd; (second row) Nick Beer, Loretta (Wilkin) Wessling, Frances Winkler, Margaret (Winkler) Lake, Margaret (Hemker) Varel, and Wilomine (Pingsterhaus) Loepker; (third row) Aloys Beer, Martin Eversgerd, Alvin Schroeder, Benny Hemker, and Bill Pingsterhaus. (Both courtesy of Carolyn Beer.)

This is a picture of the inside of a typical country school. Many of the children had to walk at least one mile to and from school. There were no bathrooms—only an outhouse. There was also no electricity, but a large furnace-style stove heated the school with coal. Suzanne Steffens is the Woodlane School teacher in this photograph from 1954. The students are shown from front to back, starting at left as follows: (first row) Dan Langenhorst, Jerome Langenhorst, Dennis Rickhoff, and Don Rickhoff; (second row) Jeanette Korte, Ron Albers, Dan Albers, and Harold Albers; (third row) Richard Albers, Fran Korte, Bob Albers, Marcel Langenhorst, and Cathy Holtmann; (fourth row) Ken Albers, JoAnn Holtmann, Martha Olliges, Carol Korte, Joe Langenhorst, and Ruth Rickhoff; (fifth row) Herb Langenhorst, Randy Albers, Linda Holtmann, Ron Korte, Rich Korte, and Kathleen Beckmann; (sixth row) David Beckman, Eugene Albers, Doris Olliges, and Pat Korte. (Courtesy of Joe Langenhorst and David Beckman.)

Above is photograph from around 1940 of the inside of the one-room Woodlane School. Henry Weirick was the teacher. Below is another Woodlane class from 1925. When remembering school days at the country school, one former student recalled, "those were the days of milking cows before school [and] chopping wood and hauling coal after. We carried our lunches of sausage and jelly sandwiches on homemade bread in molasses buckets. Children often walked a mile and a half each day to school, even on cold winter days. And those were the days when a whack on the back with a willow stick meant business." (Above, courtesy of Joe Langenhorst; below, courtesy of Marilyn Holtmann.)

In August 2008, the village of Germantown began laying another sewer line on Sycamore Street. It began from the Breese-Germantown Road and went west to State Route 161. The project was completed in October 2008. The first sewer system was built in 1956, and it is still in service. (Courtesy of Carolyn Beer.)

This 1933 photograph shows St. Boniface Catholic Church decorated for the centennial celebration. Although it was a cold, rainy day, many people came to the celebration. The outdoor altar on the north side of the church was where mass was celebrated. Church Street runs straight to the church, and Munster Street is the cross street.

J.T. Welling's hardware store was located on the corner of Main and Prairie Streets. This photograph from the 1930s shows the type of streetlights in Germantown at that time. Each evening, a man with a long pole walked to each light and used the pole to flip the switch that turned on the light. (Courtesy of John Duncan.)

These seven friends are standing in front of Lakenburges's garage. The photograph was taken in 1936, when the garage still faced Elm Street. From left to right are Martha Rensing, Lukes Lakenburges, Mary Alice Haake, Fred Rensing, Marie Mueller, Carl Schlarmann, and Toots Lakenburges. (Courtesy of Edna Lakenburges.)

These little girls are the grandchildren of Herman and Christine Robben. They are playing with puppies in the Robbens' yard in 1918. From left to right are (first row) Vivian Robben, unidentified, Alice Schoendienst, Eleanor Robben, and MaryAnn Robben; (second row) Bernice Schoendienst, Marcella Robben, Mildred Schoendienst, and Florence Robben; (third row) Marie Schoendienst, Evelyn Schoendienst, Mary Jane Schoendienst (infant), and Dolores Schoendienst. (Courtesy of Carolyn Santel.)

Henry "Hank" Eversgerd became synonymous with the IGA store in Germantown. This store was commonly known as "Hank's." Eversgerd had several jobs before the store. When he was a boy, he earned his first money opening gates for men hauling walnut logs. Later, Hank hauled cows to the stockyards in St. Louis, hauled eggs to a restaurant in East St. Louis, and made and sold century stone. (Courtesy of Shirley Eversgerd.)

These little girls are having a good time playing "wedding" in a photograph that was taken in about 1946. The little girl in front is Pat Dierkes. The girls in the back, from left to right, are as follows: Carolyn (Dierkes) Santel, Joan (Schlautmann) Schroeder, Mary Jane "Mutz" (Robke) Loepker, Jacquelyn "Mary" Schlautmann, Helen (Diesen) Wuebbles, and Angie (Schlautmann) Spirek. (Courtesy of Carolyn Santel.)

South of the beautiful crucifixion group at St. Boniface Cemetery is the old cemetery. The location of the cemetery was moved from the churchyard to Sycamore Street after the cholera scourge of 1850. Much of Germantown's history can be learned here. The eastern part of the graveyard is named Children's Cemetery. Numerous graves of young children and babies who died because of illnesses or during childbirth are located there.

This photograph from the 1950s shows an aerial view of the church grounds. St. Boniface Catholic Church is on the left, and the old grade school is on the right. Buses near the school building and other activity indicate that school has let out. The building to the southeast of the church is the convent. (Courtesy of Tom Lampe.)

On Good Friday, St. Boniface Catholic Church holds a Way of the Cross service outdoors at the cemetery. The German inscription under each station is read to remind residents of the town's German heritage. This photograph was taken in 2010 and shows Ben Lampe (left) and Dea. Richard Bagby. (Courtesy Carolyn Beer.)

Fr. Bernard Eppmann posed with this eighth-grade graduating class of 1940. The children are, from left to right, as follows: (first row) Marie Timmermann, Acklynn Fauke, Julie Vandeloo, Father Eppmann, Louis Haar, Ruth Winter, and Mary Ann Robben; (second row) George Henken, Verena Gramann, Mildred Wildhaber, Johanna Hilmes, Clara Winter, Helen Hemann, Sylvia Lehrter, Loretta Bruns, and Tracy Haar; (third row) Richard Pille, Arnold Michels, Hubert Eversgerd, Delmer Diesen, Richard Jansen, Herman Frerker, Pete Linnemann, Matthew Netemeyer, and Jim Mollet. (Courtesy of Ann Albers.)

In 1988, the Cornerstone Bar and Grill did some remodeling. As part of the project, a shed had to be torn down. It was discovered that the shed was actually a log cabin. It had bars on the windows and a large lock for the door. In all likelihood, it was used as storage for whiskey and spirits. (Courtesy of Mary Ann Jansen.)

Three

TRADITIONS, CUSTOMS, AND ARCHITECTURE

Drei Könige is a German tradition carried on in Germantown on the Feast of the Three Kings, also known as Epiphany. A small group would visit homes and perform the routine. It was customary for the household to offer the performers refreshments and wine. Pictured above in 1998, the following performers are, from left to right, Deb Nettles, Carolyn Beer, Shirley Eversgerd, Jim "Stix" Lampe, "Smiley" Haake, "Skeets" Holtmann, and Jennifer Ades. The clown in front is Dave Lampe. (Courtesy of Carolyn Beer.)

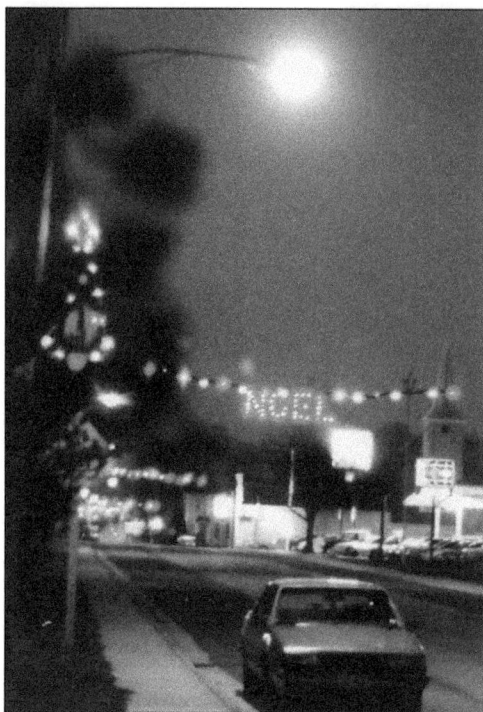

Like many cities and towns, Germantown decorates its streets with lights at Christmas. This is a photograph of a street scene at night taken in 1994. A warm Noel greets visitors during the yuletide season as they enter the town. The scene looks north up Munster Street from Highway 161. (Courtesy of Joan Young.)

Many traditional Christmas carols originated in Germany. In Germantown, carolers walked through neighborhoods and sang Christmas carols as they visited homes. It was customary for each household to offer the group refreshments. In a photograph from the 1970s, these happy friends, from left to right, are Jim Toennies, Marlene (Seelhoefer) Toennies, Mary (Brandmeyer) Toennies, Ronald "Dickie" Winkler, Barb (Neff) Voss, Regis Voss, and Carolyn (Pingsterhaus) Winkler. (Courtesy of Regis and Barb Voss.)

During the 1983 Christmas Midnight Mass, a Christmas pageant was held. Since it was Germantown's sesquicentennial year, the children dressed as early settlers. They are, from left to right, (young children on inside row) Mary Haake, John Haake, and Patti Haake; (outside row) Gwen Haake, Dan Voss, Mark Pingsterhaus, Molly Boeckmann, Christy Haake, Leah Boeckmann, Keith Hemker, Ruthann Boeckmann, Mark Mueller, and Gary Nordhaus. (Courtesy of Barb Voss.)

A church tradition that was held every three years was a visit from the bishop of the Belleville diocese to St. Boniface Catholic Church, where he would administer the sacrament of Confirmation. Pictured here are students from sixth, seventh, and eighth grade at Germantown Elementary School in 1969. Fr. Francis Seyer is standing on the left, and Sr. Mary Paulindus is standing on the right. (Courtesy of Dorothy "Susie" Holtmann.)

A tradition in the Catholic faith is Midnight Mass on Christmas Eve. Above is a 1955 photograph of mass being celebrated at St. Boniface Catholic Church. The parish priest at that time was Fr. John Boomkens. Midnight Mass is a special event in the church, and sometimes it involved a long procession by many servers wearing ceremonial cassocks. Below, some of the servers pictured are, from left to right, Dan Schwierjohn (standing next to Fr. John Boomkens), Fred Brockmann, unidentified, Gerald Eversgerd, Ralph Husmann, and Regis Voss. Stan Heideman is the server kneeling in the foreground. (Both courtesy of Regis and Barb Voss.)

St. Boniface Catholic Church holds its annual church picnic in July to help raise funds for the church. Years ago, church picnic dates among the small towns in Clinton County would sometimes conflict. In the 1930s, Herman Dierkes Sr. was with the original committee that selected the date for the picnic, and the committee decided to have the St. Boniface Catholic Church picnic on the last Tuesday in July. It has been on that day ever since. The picnic has probably been held since the early 1890s. In its early days, people donated vegetables from their gardens for the church picnic dinner, and each farmer was required to donate 10 chickens, which were then killed and plucked by hand. Some people arrived by old Model A or Model T Fords, and others traveled to town via horse and buggy. Even today, relatives return home for the picnic. Many visitors come for the delicious country fried chicken dinner and a chance to win a beautiful hand-stitched quilt. (Courtesy of Carolyn Beer.)

This pecan tree practically fills the backyard of John and Ralph Frerker. It is the oldest and largest tree in town and is located on the corner of Sycamore and Hanover Streets. This photograph was taken in 2004. One of the lower branches is so long and heavy that to prevent it from breaking, it must be held up by a prop. (Courtesy of Carolyn Beer.)

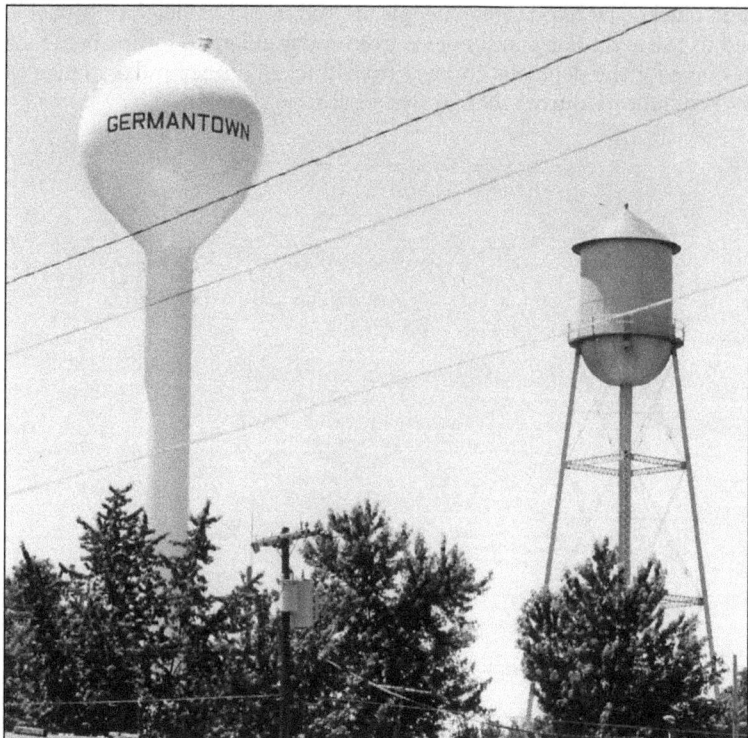

If visitors need to know what town they're in, they should just look up. The Germantown water tower is one of the town's landmarks. This photograph was taken right before workers began taking down the old water tower in 1988. It was built after the Welling Manufacturing Company burned in 1910. (Courtesy of Carolyn Beer.)

Sometimes rural places have a town dog. Sam was Germantown's dog during the 1960s. He was simply a stray dog that had become friends with many residents and was well known by the people of the community. Sam knew where to go for food, when the children got out of school, where to sleep, who liked him, and who didn't. (Courtesy of Connie Kampwerth.)

The Shoal Creek Bridge has been a Germantown landmark for many years. It was replaced in 1986. State Route 161 runs along the southern outskirts of town and crosses the bridge. It was built in 1934 using horses and wagons. Ground was borrowed from several locations to build up the present highway, thus creating pits or ponds. These became known as borrow pits and are now commonly called bar pits. (Courtesy of Barb and Regis Voss.)

The Dramatic Club was a group of local actors who performed for the community. The cast members for this play are shown from left to right as follows: (first row) Hilda Dierkes, Pete Meier, Catherine Lampe, Dave Schlarmann, and Joe Duncan; (second row) unidentified, Laura Schoendienst, Henry Lampe, Gertrude Schlarmann, Cecilia Schurmann, Frank Schurmann, Herman Schoendienst, Ann Frerker, and teacher Mr. Boyer; (third row) Ben Lampe, Felix Robke, Ted Haar Sr., and Edward Heidemann. (Courtesy of Maurice Dierkes.)

Today, many hunt game for sport. But there was a time when people depended upon it for their food. Often, hunters would give or sell their kills to friends and neighbors. These two friends have returned from a rabbit hunt in 1930. They are Jerry Frerker (left) and George Dierkes. (Courtesy of Carolyn Santel.)

The Holtmann Brothers was the first all-brother band in Germantown. The brothers were playing together as early as 1930. Pictured here from left to right are Aloys Holtmann (saxophone), Frank Holtmann (guitar), Ed Holtmann (saxophone), Lawrence Holtmann (drums), and John Holtmann (concertina). They were a popular band in the area and gave many performances. (Courtesy of Dorothy "Susie" Holtmann.)

The Commercial History of Germantown, Illinois, written in 1913, states, "It is contemplated by the young men of the city to erect a hall opposite the railroad depot, for the purpose of holding dances and affairs of pleasure during the winter season." People in Germantown have become accustomed to Sunday afternoon dances. This 1943 announcement advertises a "Married Folks Dance" to be held at the Commercial Club. (Courtesy of Dorothy "Susie" Holtmann.)

MARRIED
FOLKS DANCE

AT THE C. C. HALL
GERMANTOWN

Wednesday, Jan. 20

MUSIC BY   1943

HOLTMANN BROS.

In 1932, children received First Holy Communion in the second grade, and in the sixth grade, they had their Solemn Communion. Shown here, from left to right, are Edna (Mueller) Lakenburges and twin sister Virginia with their candle carriers, and Mary Ann Holtmann and Lucille Eilermann standing in the back. The candle carriers were often family members or relatives who carried candles in a procession, placing them on the altar for a communicant. (Courtesy of Edna Lakenburges.)

A church custom in the early 1900s was the May Day celebration at St. Boniface Catholic Church. It was the feast day honoring the Blessed Virgin Mary. There was a procession of young women dressed in white. Upon their shoulders was a platform with a statue of the Blessed Virgin. Before marching into the church, the procession stopped at the porch of the priest's house and at the convent for a benediction. (Courtesy of John Duncan.)

Taken in the 1940s, this picture shows an old poplar tree located in the St. Boniface churchyard that has grown around the wrought-iron fence surrounding the yard. This photograph also shows Munster Street. Across the street was the market that was once owned by T.W. Schlarmann, Germantown's blind butcher. (Courtesy of John Duncan.)

The Big Event
CLOSING DANCE
At the Village Park
GERMANTOWN
Given by the Germantown Fire Dept.
SUNDAY
AUG. 21
Music by Southern Illinois' popular dance band
BOOTS WILLHAUK AND HIS ORCHESTRA
Featuring a Girl Singer · · · "With Melodies that Will Linger on"
Come out and hear the finest dance band Germantown has had in years

Special $5.00 Award
Five Dollars will be awarded to the Lucky One entering the park. No charge. Get your FREE TICKETS at entrance. Something for Nothing.

Refreshments of all kinds

For Sunday, August 21st, mark your date book:
"THE VILLAGE PARK"
Koch Printers, Germantown

A popular form of entertainment in Germantown in the 1930s was the platform dance. This poster advertises the final dance at the Village Park, which was located behind the fire department building on Prairie Street. Large boards on the ground served as a dance platform. The dances were held to raise money for the community. (Courtesy of Dave Neff.)

At left, these outfits may look like dresses but they are not. They are swimming suits! In the early 1900s, a young lady had to wear long stockings when in public, even when swimming. Many suits were knee-length wool dresses complete with lace-up swimming slippers and fancy caps. Here, Veronica Welling (right) and a friend are taking a dip on a hot afternoon in Shoal Creek. Below is a picture of Welling playing tennis. There was a tennis court north of town. Both the swimming suits and tennis outfit are quite different from what is worn today. (Both courtesy of John and Florence Duncan.)

The Germantown Spassfest featured the local Boomkessel Band. The novelty band appeared regularly at the Spassfest for 35 years. Always a crowd-pleaser, the band held sing-alongs and performed German folk songs. Literally, the German word *boomkessel* means "noise kettle." A *boomkessel* was actually a long pole, held upright, that held a cymbal, tin plate, bicycle horn, tar bucket, and two brass Model A Ford headlight reflectors. In the early years, the Boomkessel Band went on the road promoting the annual Spassfest and even appeared on television. Boomkessel instrument player Dave Lampe became a symbol for the group. This photograph from 1968 shows the original members of the band. Pictured from left to right are (first row) Pete Robke and Ken Buenemeyer; (second row) Don Frerker, Gene Hilmes, and Dave Lampe. The band has had other members through the years, including Mary Ann Korte on snare drums and Tom Lampe on the keyboard. (Courtesy of Joe Langenhorst.)

Helping to preserve some of the history of Germantown is Pete Linnemann, who lives with his wife, Lorraine, on the corner of Mill and Elm Streets. He has dedicated himself to preserving Germantown's history by painstakingly constructing the town as it looked years ago. Often, he uses a photograph as a guide, but many times he relies on his own memory. This photograph was taken in 2008 at the town's quartoseptcentennial celebration. (Courtesy of John Skain.)

Germans influenced many traditions, such as coloring eggs and the Easter Bunny. Germantown's annual Easter egg hunt takes place at the St. Boniface churchyard. Children hurry to be the first to pick up the eggs and candy. Years ago, live chicks and baby rabbits were also on hand, and the grand prize was a young lamb. This picture was taken in the 1960s.

Peddlers often came to town, especially during the Great Depression. Back then, the term "hobo" was used to denote someone who was homeless, out of work, and rode in railroad boxcars from town to town. One such peddler was called the "Umbrella Man." Another peddler who frequented the area sharpened knives and tools. This is a photograph of Mrs. Duke, a peddler who went through towns fixing typewriters and sewing machines.

In Germany, it was customary for houses or barns to have inscriptions marking the year the family farm was established. This photograph was taken in 2009 and shows the original Niebur farm located on Highway 161, just west of Germantown. Rose, Joseph Niebur's daughter, built a house on the property in 1915. Above the porch, she carried on the German custom with the inscription "B. BY. R.N. 1915," meaning the house was built by Rose Niebur in 1915.

CHOLERA CROSS

IN 1832 CHOLERA PLAGUED THIS AREA
ENTIRE FAMILIES WERE WIPED OUT,
SOMETIMES OVER NIGHT
JOS ALTEPETER MADE A COVENANT
WITH HIS MAKER, IF HIS LARGE FAMILY
WAS SPARED HE WOULD ERECT
A LARGE CROSS ON HIS FARM
NEAR THE PUBLIC ROAD AS A
PERPETUAL MEMORIAL
THE FAMILY WAS SPARED AND
THE ORIGINAL WOODEN CROSS THAT
WAS BUILT HAS BEEN
REPLACED MANY TIMES.

Much of the architecture in and around Germantown reminds residents of history. Above, one of the most impressive reminders of the days of the cholera plague is located at the Timmerman farm, which is about three miles from Germantown along the Breese-Germantown Road. The devastating cholera plague occurred after the Black Hawk War in 1832. The cross was erected by Henry Altepeter, one of the original settlers to emigrate from Germany. He prayed for his family to be spared from the illness and promised to erect a cross on his land if they were. The original wooden cross has been replaced several times and is now made of concrete. At left, a plaque that describes some of the history of the cholera plague is located at the base of the cross. There were many horror stories. The disease spread like a prairie fire and no one survived the disease once they contracted it.

A popular event at the St. Boniface Catholic Church picnic is the quilt bingo. Several ladies work year-round making handmade quilts. The women shown here are busily stitching quilts for the 2011 church picnic. They quilt every Tuesday morning at the church rectory. They appear from front to back as follows: (left row) Lorraine Linnemann, Alice Pingsterhaus, Christine Beckmann, and Lorene Fauke; (right row) Esther Dierkes, Martha Duing, Edna Lakenburges, and Marilyn Haake. (Photograph by Rena Haake.)

In keeping with the German tradition of ornate clocks, Alvin "Abby" Albers, one of Germantown's oldest residents, handcrafts these beautiful items as a hobby. Albers and his wife, Henrietta, live on Leo Street. He carefully traces intricate patterns onto thin pieces of plywood using carbon paper. He then uses a scroll saw to meticulously cut out each pattern. This 2010 photograph shows one of his many clocks. (Courtesy of Abby Albers.)

Many aspects of German heritage are still evident in Germantown. Donut Ditch is one of them. This ditch begins north of town, runs under the mill, turns at Walnut Street, and runs along the side of Hanover Street. It empties into a borrow pit. Today, most of the ditch is underground, but until the 1950s, it was a large, open ditch. In the spring, this ditch would often flood when the water rose at Shoal Creek. It sometimes flooded as far as Walnut Street. The town's ancestors called the trench the Donau Ditch for the German word that refers to the Danube River, which is a major waterway that runs through several countries in Europe, including Germany, and floods regularly. As time went on and more and more residents stopped speaking German, the word Donau became misconstrued and the slang word for the ditch became "donut." Hanover Street was commonly called Donut Road.

On October 27, 1948, Gerald Jansen and Margaret Fruth were married. After a wedding ceremony, the servers would hold up a wedding cord so the bride and groom could not leave the church without paying them first. In those days, people got married on a weekday. The daylong celebration began with a wedding mass and breakfast in the morning, wedding cake and coffee in the afternoon, and a dinner and dance in the evening.

Another tradition during the 1940s and 1950s was straw dummies. Before a wedding, these were hung as a joke played on the jilted lover. Often, the display included a sign with a humorous verse. This straw dummy was hung at the corner of Sycamore Street and Munster Street. The rooftops of Fred Bohnkemper's house and Vince Wessling's tavern on Munster Street can be seen below the dummy. (Courtesy of Tom Lampe.)

A letter from some visitors to Germantown dated 1859 reads, "Most of the houses are well built with fencing, railings, etc. that are kept in good repair. The narrowness of the streets, however, must ever be a serious objection to the place." The picture above shows the architecture of the streets. The town's German ancestors were used to the narrow streets of the villages in Germany. Although the picture of Elm Street below was taken in 2010, the narrowness of the roads is still evident. On a recent visit, a former resident of Germantown commented with surprise that he did not remember the roads being so narrow.

Several homes in Germantown reflect Old World architecture. As shown above, many are typical German wood-frame houses with a pointed dormer that is sometimes decorated with ornate molding at the point. They often have front porches with ornate molding as well. Some of the houses still have double front doors. One door led to the parlor, and the other door was the entrance to the bedroom and other living quarters. Today, they are commonly known as funeral doors. Until the late 1940s, there were no commercial funeral homes in town. Instead, funeral wakes were held in private homes. The home in the photograph below was built by Joseph Niebur in 1888. It still stands today on Sycamore Street. Shown from left to right are (first row) Sr. Mary Bernadine and Sr. Mary Boniface; (second row) Frances Gesenhues and Rose Niebur.

There were many local Christmas traditions handed down from German ancestors. Germantown always celebrated the Feast of Saint Nicholas. Groups would often go "Nicholas-ing" on December 6. One person dressed as Saint Nicholas and carried a flour sack or pillowcase full of popcorn. He had a dark-faced companion called Black Peter who represented the devil and rattled a chain. The duo would visit the homes of families with children and Saint Nicholas would ask, "*Kannst du beten?*" which means "Can you pray?" If the children did not pray, Black Peter threatened to chain them to a tree. The children who prayed got popcorn and candy. Another local tradition was *Thuene Schein* (the spelling and meaning are uncertain). It occurred after Christmas. A group would take a decorated Christmas tree and throw it at the front door or set it on the porch of a friend's house. The group would then hide. When the homeowner answered the door, he or she would have to find the group. When the group was located, everyone went into the house for a holiday party.

Germantown's village hall is located on Prairie Street. This photograph shows the town's logo, an illustration of leaves, at the top of this sign located outside village hall. The leaves represent the linden trees that were brought from Germany. They serve as a reminder of the strength, integrity, and determination of Germantown's ancestors. (Courtesy of Dorothy "Susie" Holtmann.)

In the late 1930s, a flood and mud slide washed out the railroad track between the third and fourth railroad trestles east of town. Station hands had to repair it. The water got up as high as the bridge. This photograph shows workers shoveling rock from a railroad car in order to build up the track. (Courtesy of Dave Lampe.)

What do the Germantown Savings Bank (above) and Ski soda (below) have in common? In May 1928, a robbery took place at the bank. Ed "Lefty" Meier was delivering ice cream to Lehrter's ice cream parlor on Main Street and got a good look at the robbers. Since he could describe the men to the police, they apprehended the criminals and Lefty received a substantial reward. He used the reward to begin the Excel Bottling Company, which is located in Breese, Illinois. Ski soda is a very popular soda in Germantown and Clinton County. Though it can now be bought from stores in cans and is artificially flavored, Excel Bottling Company still uses pure cane sugar and bottles. Anyone in Germantown can tell you that there is nothing like the refreshing taste of a bottled Ski from Excel Bottling Company. (Above, courtesy of James Lampe Sr., below, courtesy of Cathy Williams.)

In 1983, Germantown celebrated its sesquicentennial, marking 150 years as a village. As part of the celebration, there was a costume contest during which residents dressed as settlers. In the photograph above, the winners of the contest were, from left to right, (first row) Dean Korte and Matt Korte; (second row) Tim Korte (infant), Dan Korte, Vickie Korte, Anne Frerker, Gerald Jansen, Mary Ann Jansen, and Gene Robke. In 2008, Germantown celebrated its quartoseptcentennial, marking its 175th year. There were several events throughout the year, including a street fair and a parade in the summer. The photograph below shows the Golden Keg of beer. During the 2008 celebration, the mayor toasted the town's German ancestors. (Above, courtesy of Mary Ann Jansen, below, courtesy of Carolyn Beer.)

Germantown proudly celebrates its German heritage every summer in mid-August at the annual Spassfest (German for "fun fest"). Since it began in 1968, the Spassfest has been a total community effort that benefits the entire town. The event was initiated as a means of raising funds for a park and other community improvement projects. The Spassfest is still held today, and its longevity can be attributed to the many volunteers who work very hard for its success. The event is held in the park located at the east end of Sycamore Street. The Spassfest has always been known for its authentic German food and the polka mass celebrated at St. Boniface Catholic Church. Additionally, the festival includes rides, games, music, a German *biergarten* (beer garden), and plenty of fun. (Both courtesy of Vicky Albers.)

Four

TAKE ME OUT
TO THE BALL GAME

The Centrals won eight games and lost three in 1911. This photograph was taken at Steiling's baseball field, which was located northwest of Germantown. The members of the team were, from left to right, (first row) George Eisele, unidentified, Louis Schoendienst, unidentified, and Herman Schoendienst; (second row) Joe "Red" Schoendienst Sr., Lefty Meyer, Ed Roach, William Eisele, and unidentified. (Courtesy of Joe and Irene Schoendienst.)

The first trophy that the Germantown Baseball Club won was the Leacock trophy, pictured at left, in 1933. Louis Schoendienst, the team's mascot, proudly displays the plaque in the photograph below. For many years, it hung in the Dugout Tavern on Main Street, which was owned by Ferd Mueller. The tavern was a popular gathering place after Sunday afternoon ball games. (Courtesy of Ferd Mueller.)

In 1933, the Germantown Baseball Club won the Clinton County league championship. The proud county champs are shown, from left to right, as follows: (first row) George Schlautmann, Vincent "Pete" Meyer, Harold Hummel, Louis Schoendienst (mascot), Rod Hang, Louis Lakenburges, and Frank Shermann; (second row) Joe Schoendienst, E.P. Roach, John Schoendienst, Lawrence Huser, Paul Schoendienst, August Heidemann, Ed Hemann, William Damerich, Lloyd Hellmann, and L.J. Schoendienst. (Courtesy of Edna Lakenburges.)

The 1929 baseball club posed for a group picture next to the old school south of St. Boniface Catholic Church. They are, from left to right, (first row) Burt Werth, Mock "Shippy" Schurmann, Pete Meyer, Lawrence Huser, and Joe Lager; (second row) Louis Schoendienst, Gus Heidemann, Eddie Hoosier, Ed Hemann, Truman "Posey" Orell, Eddie Schniers, and Aloys Heidemann. (Courtesy of Ferd Mueller.)

This is the Germantown Baseball Club from the 1940s. The following players are shown from left to right: (first row) unidentified, Lukes Lakenburges, Pete Meier, Charlie Schoendienst, Harold Hummel, Ed Schniers, and ? Boevingloh; (second row) Joe Schoendienst (umpire), Gus Heideman, Ed Hoag, Eddie Hoosier, Earl Taylor, Paul Schoendienst, two unidentified players, Louis Schoendienst, and Ed Roach. (Courtesy of Joe and Irene Schoendienst.)

Bartelso Lumber & Supply Co.

Let us Solve Your Building & Remodelling Problems

Complete Line of Quality Building Materials   DeLaval Milkers and Coolers
Cabinets, Screens, etc. made to order   Expert Landscaping Service

Brefeld Funeral Parlor
GERMANTOWN

Free Ambulance Service to Local Hospital
Aviston Phone: No. 16 or 26   Germantown phone ordered to be installed

SCORE-CARD
Germantown Baseball Club
1950

BRUEGGE
FUNERAL HOME
GERMANTOWN AND BREESE

Hanover Star
Milling Company

Phone 41

Germantown - Illinois

Compliments of

Germantown
Commercial
Club

This baseball scorecard is from 1950. These were used when raising money for a new grandstand at Haake's baseball field. This field is now called Schoendienst Field and is located in the park where the annual Spassfest is held. The people of Germantown dedicated the field to their native son Red Schoendienst in 1979. (Courtesy of Ferd Mueller.)

The Germantown Trades won the league championship in 1951. Members of the baseball club are, from left to right, (first row) Frank Schoendienst, David Neff, Elmer Schoendienst, Smiley Haake, and John Frerker; (second row) Joe Schoendienst, Spike Haake, Ray Boeckmann, Leroy Haukap, Lou Winter, Homer Hilmes, Bob Haake, and Ben Buenemeyer. (Courtesy of Joe and Irene Schoendienst.)

Wobbe's pasture was one of the early ball fields where Germantown played baseball. It was located southwest of town. During the week, it was a farmer's pasture. Cows would graze there and sometimes had to be chased off the field before the game. A young James Jansen (right) and his friend Joe Schoendienst (left) often laid down the ball stripes before the games.

In 1966, the Dutchmans, another Germantown Baseball Club, were league champions. Pictured from left to right are (first row) Frank Richter, Frank Schlautmann, Jerry Von Atter, Gary Kohrman (bat boy), Bob Haake, Dale Ades, and Stan Heidemann; (second row) Alfie Mensing, Bernie Schlarmann, Albert Haake, Alan Thoele, Paul Jansen, Gene Heidemann, Leroy Diesen, Len Robben, Rich Haake, Laverne Korte, Ron Haake, and Gus Heidemann. (Courtesy of Ferd Mueller.)

In 1983, as part of Germantown's 150th anniversary, there was an old-timers baseball game. Former players came to play ball in their old uniforms. Shown are, from left to right, Leroy Dierkes (uniform from the early 1970s), Gene Heideman (uniform from the 1960s), Leroy Haukap (uniform from the 1948–1950 baseball seasons), Alan Thoele (uniform from 1972), Stix Lampe (uniform from the 1980s), Dan Schwierjohn (uniform from 1964), and Ferd Mueller (sesquicentennial clothes). (Courtesy of Ferd Mueller.)

Germantown was crazy about baseball. People would gather around the radio at the Fruth Brothers' Garage to listen to the ball game. On Sundays, Gerald Jansen would pump gas at Jansen Chevrolet Company in his uniform so he wouldn't be late for the game. In this 1936 photograph, Gerald is standing on Locust Street next to Jansen's garage and in front of the bus he drove. (Courtesy of Dave Jansen.)

Albert "Red" Schoendienst is a former player for the St. Louis Cardinals and a former coach and manager for the team. He played, coached, or managed in nine World Series. He played in 10 all-star games and managed the National League squad in two games. In 1989, he was inducted into the Baseball Hall of Fame in Cooperstown, New York. Although he spent much of his life in St. Louis with the Cardinals, he has fond memories of growing up in Germantown, a place where, as he recalls, he would rather go hunting or swimming in the Old Shoal Creek than go to school. He began playing baseball in Germantown when he was a teenager and played with men twice his age at Wobbe's pasture and at the park that would later be dedicated to him. He watched Ed Roach manage his baseball teams and learned from him. Schoendienst is an icon for the little town of Germantown, and he inspires many. (Courtesy of Sue Britton.)

Albert "Red" Schoendienst was born on February 2, 1923. He was raised in a typical German home in Germantown on the corner of Walnut and Elm Streets. The house faced east. His father, Joe Schoendienst Sr., was a catcher for Germantown's baseball team. Later, Joe was an umpire. Sons Joe and Red Schoendienst remember when their father would work in the coal mine all day and then umpire a baseball game after work. (Courtesy of Joe and Irene Schoendienst.)

In a picture taken in the 1940s for a local newspaper, the Schoendienst boys pose in their baseball uniforms. While Red Schoendienst played in the major leagues for the St. Louis Cardinals, each of his brothers played for the minor leagues within the Cardinals' organization. Shown, from left to right, are Red; Julius, who played for a minor league team in Columbus, Ohio; Elmer, who played for a team in Duluth, Minnesota; and Joe, who played for a team in Johnson City, Tennessee. (Courtesy of Stella Schoendienst Jeffries.)

In 1989, Albert "Red" Schoendienst was inducted into the National Hall of Fame Museum in Cooperstown, New York. The plaque at right reads, "Roommate Stan Musial credited him with 'the greatest pair of hands I've ever seen.' Sleek, far-ranging second baseman for 18 seasons, led NL in fielding and hit .300 or better seven times. When elected in 1989, he had worn a major league uniform 45 consecutive seasons as player, coach, and manager, piloting the Redbirds to World Series in 1967 and 1968. 14th inning homer won the 1950 All-Star Game for the NL." Shown below, in 1979, Germantown honored Red by naming the town's baseball field after him. The Germantown Park District maintains a memorial site, complete with a red bench. The memorial has a replica of the hall of fame plaque. (Right, courtesy of Ferd Mueller; below, courtesy of Diane Schniers.)

ALBERT FRED SCHOENDIENST
"RED"
ST. LOUIS, N.L., 1945-1956, 1961-1963
NEW YORK, N.L., 1956-1957
MILWAUKEE, N.L., 1957-1960
ROOMMATE STAN MUSIAL CREDITED HIM WITH "GREATEST PAIR OF HANDS I'VE EVER SEEN". SLEEK, FAR-RANGING SECOND BASEMAN FOR 18 SEASONS. LED N.L. IN FIELDING AND HIT .300 OR BETTER SEVEN TIMES. WHEN ELECTED IN 1989 HAD WORN MAJOR LEAGUE UNIFORM 45 CONSECUTIVE SEASONS AS PLAYER, COACH AND MANAGER. PILOTING REDBIRDS TO WORLD SERIES IN 1967 AND 1968. 14TH INNING HOMER WON 1950 ALL-STAR GAME FOR N.L.

In the picture at left from April 11, 1999, a sculpture was unveiled to honor Red Schoendienst. It is located outside Busch Memorial Stadium in St. Louis, Missouri, at 100 South Fourth Street. Below, the plaque on the bottom of the sculpture reads, "This statue shows one of baseball's best-fielding second basemen turning a double play in the mid-1940s. Red served as a major league player, coach and manager from 1945 to 1995 and a special assistant to the general manager. Red managed the Cardinals for 12 years—a Cardinals Club record. He hit .300 seven times in his career and accumulated 2,449 hits. He was a lifetime .289 hitter, and was chosen to 10 all-star teams. He was inducted into baseball's Hall of Fame in 1989." (Both photographs by Robert F. Sager.)

RED SCHOENDIENST
UNVEILED APRIL 11, 1999

This statue shows one of baseball's best-fielding second basemen turning a double play in the mid 1940's. Red served as a Major League player, coach and manager from 1945-95 and as a special assistant to the general manager. Red managed the Cardinals for 12 years—a Cardinals Club record. He hit .300 seven times in his career and accumulated 2,449 hits. He was a lifetime .289 hitter, and was chosen to ten All-Star teams. He was inducted into baseball's Hall of Fame in 1989.

Five

PROUDLY WE SERVE

On October 15, 2006, Germantown celebrated the dedication of the Veterans Memorial Park with a mass at St. Boniface Catholic Church and a parade down the village streets. Shown at the podium is the current mayor of Germantown, Gerald Kohnen. Seated beside him is parish priest Fr. Steve Humphrey and Congressman John Shimkus. Seated in front of the stage is Gold Star Mother Irma Eversgerd, who lost two sons in the Vietnam War. (Courtesy of John Skain.)

Above, the Veterans War Memorial stands as a witness to the town's strong foundation and values. The memorial includes flags from the various branches of military service. It was constructed on the shore of Germantown's beautiful lake and park, which are located on Munster Street next to State Route 161 south of town. Below, a closer view of the memorial shows a large obelisk. The inscription reads, "We dedicate this memorial to the courage and valor of the members of our community who served this country by answering the call to freedom." The monument is surrounded by bricks inscribed with the names of veterans who have served the United States. (Both courtesy of Carolyn Beer.)

During the Civil War, 34 young men from Hanover enlisted and served in Company K, 30th Regiment of the Illinois Volunteer Infantry. The 30th Illinois Infantry was in the thick of battle during the entire war. This photograph was taken in 1982 at Bobby Eversgerd's fort. This stone fort is located two miles south of Highway 161 on Old Shoal Creek Road. It has a museum with Civil War and Native American artifacts. (Courtesy of Dorothy "Susie" Holtmann.)

Boy Scout Troop No. 73 gathered at the American Legion home in 1957 for this photograph. The Scouts are, from left to right, (first row) Tom Deien, Wayne Robke, Fred Brockmann, Roger Haukap, and Laverne Kohnen; (second row) George Dierkes (assistant Scoutmaster), Fred Hemann, Eugene Heidemann, Val Eversgerd Jr., Jerry Van Atter, David Hemann, Jim Kohnen, Leroy Dierkes, and Fred Randant (Scoutmaster). (Courtesy of Carolyn Santel.)

The American Legion building was dedicated in 1953. The celebration included a mass, a parade down Sycamore Street, and a special dedication ceremony. The men carrying the flags before the Legionnaires in the front row of the parade are, from left to right, Joe Hemann, Robert Kohrman, Roger Lakenburges, and Paul Dierkes. (Courtesy of Paul Dierkes.)

Diesen-Winkler American Legion Post 325 received its charter in 1919. Anton Diesen and Conrad Winkler were the first two men from Germantown to be killed in the line of duty during World War I. This photograph shows the new American Legion building on the corner of Sycamore and West Streets in 1953. The post includes the Legionnaires, the American Legion Ladies Auxiliary, and the Sons of the American Legion. (Courtesy of Dorothy "Susie" Holtmann.)

Like many American Legion halls, the one in Germantown is host to a variety of events. This photograph was taken in 1953, when the hall was new. Since then, it has been remodeled with a kitchen, additional rooms, and a wheelchair lift. Two weekly events include Saturday night bingo and Sunday afternoon dances. They have become a tradition and attract many throughout the county. (Courtesy of Dorothy "Susie" Holtmann.)

This photograph shows the members of the Germantown American Legion drill team. They are standing in front of the American Legion in 1958 and are, from left to right, (first row) Joe Hemann, John Lakenburges, Dan Rosen, Herbert Dierkes, Bud Fauke, and Jerome Eversgerd; (second row) Elmer Diesen, Franklin Schoendienst, Harold Robben, Eugene Hilmes; (third row) unidentified, Joe Leonard, Raymond Wessling, and Donald Frerker. (Courtesy of Dan Rosen.)

Diesen-Winkler Post 325 of the American Legion in Germantown has designated a wall as a memorial to those who died in wars. The fallen veterans include T.Sgt. 5 Clarence Gramann (World War II, 6th Army Infantry, killed in Italy); Sgt. Norbert Horstmann (World War II, 180th Infantry, killed in Africa); Cpl. Lawrence Huser (World War II, 35th Regiment, killed in France); Cpl. Alfred Linnemann (World War II, 381st Infantry, killed in Okinawa, Japan); Pvt. Anton Diesen (World War I, 147th Infantry, killed in France); Pvt. George Winkler (World War I, 47th Infantry, killed in Germany); Sp4c. Marlin G. Eversgerd (22nd Infantry, killed in Vietnam); Pvt. Norman L. Eversgerd (USMC, killed in Vietnam); Cpl. Ralph B. Ortmann (1st Cavalry Division, killed in Vietnam); Cpl. Herbert Langenhorst (2nd Battalion, killed in Vietnam); and S.Sgt. Josh A. Melton (Operation Enduring Freedom, killed in Afghanistan).

In 1968, Diesen-Winkler Post 325 of the American Legion in Germantown celebrated its 50th anniversary. The photograph above shows the World War I veterans and their wives. Pictured from left to right are (first row) Elizabeth Thoele (sister of two brothers who could not attend), Agnes Leonard, Elizabeth Lampe, Frances Leonard, Mary Deerhaake, Emelia Robben, Sophie Maue, Helen Korte, Regenia Boevingloh, and Christine Beckmann; (second row) Fred Floppe, William Leonard, Henry Lampe, Ben Leonard, High Deerhaake, George Robben, Joe Maue, George Korte, Tony Boevingloh, Alphonse Beckmann, and the state commander. Shown below, as part of the entertainment for the evening, are three Legionnaires providing music. From left to right are Ben Leonard, who played the harmonica; Tony Boevingloh, who played on his arm; and Henry Lampe, who played the jug. (Both courtesy of Germantown American Legion.)

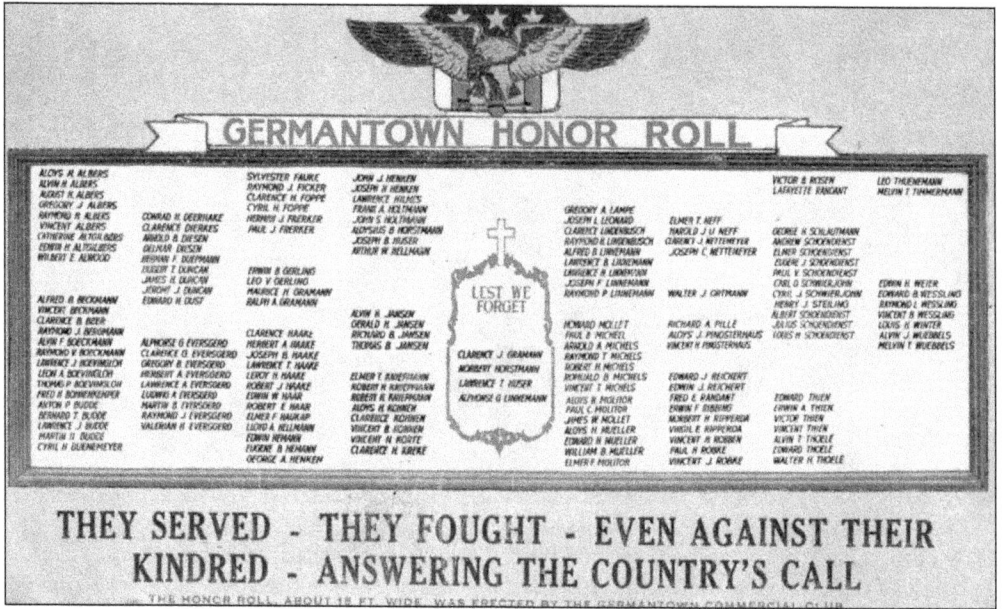

GERMANTOWN HONOR ROLL

LEST WE FORGET

THEY SERVED - THEY FOUGHT - EVEN AGAINST THEIR
KINDRED - ANSWERING THE COUNTRY'S CALL

In the 1940s, many young men in Germantown chose to enlist in the military to serve in World War II. To honor them, the town erected an honor roll. Located in the St. Boniface churchyard north of the church sidewalk, the memorial faced Munster Street. (Courtesy of Diane Schniers.)

World War II lasted from 1939 to 1945. This photograph of Pvt. Thomas B. Jansen was taken in 1944 at an Army training camp in California. Jansen was later sent to the Southwest Pacific and served in the field artillery.

The Vietnam War was America's longest war at the time. It was fought in Vietnam, Laos, and Cambodia. Taken in the late 1960s, this photograph is labeled "The Army's Three Biggest Mistakes Terrorize Saigon." These three friends from Germantown are, from left to right, Bill Fauke, Richard Kuhl, and John Schlautmann. (Courtesy of Diane Schniers.)

Each year on Memorial Day, there is a mass at St. Boniface Catholic Church and a ceremony at the cemetery to honor Germantown's veterans. This picture was taken in 2008. The man walking in front is Joe Langenhorst. The others, from left to right, are as follows: (first row) Fr. Jim Buerster and Dea. Rich Bagby (behind Langenhorst); (second row) Andrea Musenbrock, Jerome Eversgerd, Don Albers, Norbert Pingsterhaus, Dennis Loepker, and unidentified. (Courtesy of Carolyn Beer.)

The Germantown Fire Company was chartered on May 2, 1892. The first firefighting apparatus was a hand-operated pump that had to be loaded onto a horse-drawn wagon. These men stopped their work briefly to pose for a photograph. Seated on the ladder wagon (left) are, from left to right, Henry Vieth, Theodore "Toby" Hoff, and Henry Robke. Joe Haake is next to the horse. Standing in front of the next wagon, from left to right, are (first row) John Haake, Henry Thien, John Schoendienst, Herman Heet, and Herman Frerker; (second row) Ben Gerling, Herman Robben, Ben Von Boemmel, and Henry Hellman; (third row) Frank Hallermann, Ben Meyer, unidentified, and John Wiegers. Herman Ribbing is next to the horse. The Germantown Fire Department is more than 100 years old. (Courtesy of Fire Chief Jeff Johnson and the Germantown Fire Department.)

On Labor Day 1948, the Germantown Fire Company posed for a photograph with a new 1941 pumper truck. This truck was in service until 1988. The volunteers are, from left to right, (first row) Alphonse Hemann, Fire Chief Louis Lakenburges, Pete Meier, Frank Frerker, Elmer Husmann, Jack Fruth, and Barney Hermeling; (second row) B.J. Buenemeyer, Hank Eversgerd, Frank Robke, Fred Robke, Nick Beer, Henry Hemann, and Jerry Frerker. (Courtesy of Edna Lakenburges.)

The Germantown Fire Department receives tremendous support from the community through various fundraising events. It was the first fire department to have a radio system in the county. In 1983, the fire department began providing emergency medical service to the community and surrounding area. The tank pump truck shown here is one of the most recent additions to the department. (Courtesy of Fire Chief Jeff Johnson and the Germantown Fire Department.)

In the early days, funds for the Germantown Fire Department were entirely donated. In the 1930s and 1940s, platform dances were used as fundraisers. In the 1950s, the department raised enough money to build a new fire station. The old fire department bell is now a monument and serves as a reminder of the department's history. (Courtesy of Carolyn Beer.)

The Germantown Police Department was not formally created until the mid-1970s. Until then, a constable was appointed by the village to settle arguments, enforce rules, and generally keep the peace. In fact, the town constable was originally called a justice of the peace. In April 1876, Fritz Schlautmann was appointed the first village constable. This is a photograph of the badge owned by Germantown's last constable, Aloys Kohnen. (Courtesy of Village President Gerald Kohnen.)

Germantown has been honored on three separate occasions with the Governor's Home Town Award. These awards show the dedication and the resolve of the residents of Germantown. The first Governor's Home Town Award, a general award, was given in 1995 for the construction of the Germantown Public Library. In 1996, the village won first place for its involvement with youth. This award was presented to the Kernel Nut Club—an organization dedicated to the youth of Germantown—for its assistance in providing and helping the school district raise funds for marching band uniforms. In 2007, Germantown again took first place for community pride for honoring its veterans by erecting the veterans memorial. Germantown is a unique community and a wonderful place to live, work, and raise a family. People are friendly and always willing to help each other. Germantown's character and family values come from deep German roots and rich history.

Visit us at
arcadiapublishing.com

www.ingramcontent.com/pod-product-compliance
Lightning Source LLC
Chambersburg PA
CBHW050625110426
42813CB00007B/1720